PIANO PRONTO

Prelude
(Primer Level)

Music & Materials by

Jennifer Eklund

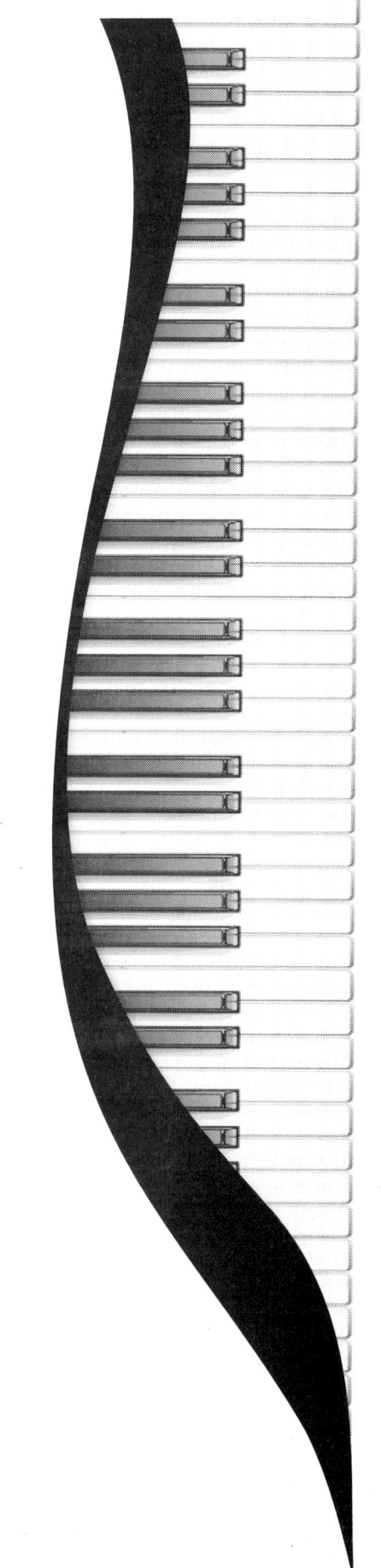

PIANO PRONTO PUBLISHING

PianoPronto.com

Piano Pronto: Prelude (2nd Edition)

Jennifer Eklund

Copyright ©2006 by Piano Pronto Publishing, Inc.
Second Edition copyright ©2015 by Piano Pronto Publishing, Inc.

All rights reserved. The compositions, arrangements, text, and graphics in this publication are protected by copyright law. No part of this work may be duplicated or reprinted without the prior consent of the author.

ISBN 978-1-942751-02-1

Printed in the United States of America.

Piano Pronto Publishing, Inc.
PianoPronto.com

Prelude
TABLE OF CONTENTS

JUST THE BASICS 3
MY FIRST STEPS *(Eklund)* 10
SONG FOR THE MOON *(Lully)* 11
MARY HAD A LITTLE LAMB *(Traditional)* 12
MY PIANO SONG *(Eklund)* 13
GOOD KING WHAT'S-HIS-FACE *(Traditional)* 14
TWINKLE, TWINKLE, LITTLE STAR *(Traditional)* 16
FARMER IN THE DELL *(Traditional)* 18
JINGLE BELLS *(Pierpont)* 20
SWEETLY SINGS THE DONKEY *(Traditional)* 22
ODE TO JOY *(Beethoven)* 24
ON YOUR TOES! *(Eklund)* 26
BROTHER JOHN *(Traditional)* 28
WESTMINSTER CHIMES *(Traditional)* 30
HOT CROSS BUNS *(Traditional)* 32
RAIN, RAIN, GO AWAY *(Traditional)* 34
RIVER ROAD *(Dvořák)* 36
MERRILY WE ROLL ALONG *(Traditional)* 38
LIGHTLY ROW *(Traditional)* 40
LONDON BRIDGE *(Traditional)* 42
ON THE BRIDGE AT AVIGNON *(Traditional)* 44
HUSH, LITTLE BABY *(Traditional)* 46
DOWN IN THE VALLEY *(Traditional)* 48
ROW, ROW, ROW YOUR BOAT *(Traditional)* 50
SKIP TO MY LOU *(Traditional)* 52
OH, SUSANNAH *(Foster)* 54
OLD MACDONALD *(Traditional)* 56
MORNING THEME *(Grieg)* 59
SNAKE DANCE *(Traditional)* 63
KITTY WALTZ *(Eklund)* 66
THE OLD GRAY MARE *(Traditional)* 68
IF YOU'RE HAPPY AND YOU KNOW IT *(Traditional)* 70
MY COUNTRY, 'TIS OF THEE *(Traditional)* 72

Note to Parents

Congratulations on your decision to give the gift of music to your child. Learning to play the piano is a fun and rewarding experience that can last a lifetime. The following tips will help ensure continued success throughout the process:

PIANO: Before beginning lessons, make sure that your child has a proper instrument to practice on. While an electronic keyboard may suffice in the very beginning, I strongly recommend renting or purchasing an acoustic instrument. Students are generally more motivated to practice on a real instrument as opposed to a keyboard, which is often perceived as a toy.

PRACTICE: Success depends on daily practice. Make an effort to include practicing the piano as a part of your child's daily routine. I recommend that students practice their assigned pieces every day, and also review previous repertoire. It is my philosophy that daily practice does not necessarily need to be completed in one long session. In fact, some of the most successful students often sit down and play for short periods several times a day. Through daily practice, your child will achieve confidence and a high comfort level with the piano.

PATIENCE & PERSISTANCE: While learning music is fun and rewarding, it is also a long and challenging process. Every student learns and progresses at a different rate, and plateaus in the learning process are unavoidable. Be sure to encourage and support your child at these inevitable sticking points. Remaining patient and persistent will ultimately yield great results!

PROUD PARENTS: Take pride in your child's music education. You do not need to have any music education yourself in order to play an important role in your child's musical development. Ask questions about the pieces your child is studying and inquire about things you see in your child's books that you are unfamiliar with—kids take great pride in teaching their parents what they are learning. Take time to sit down for "impromptu concerts" to show your child that you have an active interest in what your child is studying.

I have fond memories of my practice sessions as a child where my parents would make requests to hear their favorite pieces. While it did not dawn on me back then, I realize now that these little evening concerts from our living room subconsciously provided me the satisfaction that my hard work made a difference and was enjoyed and important to everybody in the household. In short, any positive reinforcement you can offer will help ensure the motivation and success of your child.

Note to Teachers

Thank you for choosing the Piano Pronto lesson book series for your students. I am confident you will find the material easy to follow, and that it will keep your students motivated and excited about their piano lessons.

WHO SHOULD USE THIS BOOK? The Piano Pronto *Prelude* book is intended for beginners age 10 and up, or students of all ages who have some prior experience with the piano or another musical instrument. Because of the accelerated pacing of this book I recommend that younger beginners start with the *Keyboard Kickoff* book where the pacing is a bit slower.

HOW DO I TRANSITION FROM *KEYBOARD KICKOFF*?

Standard Transition: Start at the beginning of *Prelude* right after finishing *Keyboard Kickoff*. The easy songs in the beginning of *Prelude* will serve as a review. This is a good solution for students who need a refresher or who could benefit from slowing down a bit and moving sideways for a while. Make sure to use the *Prelude: Teacher Duet Parts* to reinforce solid rhythmic skills and collaborative work.

Functional Skills Transition: Upon finishing *Keyboard Kickoff*, transition to *Prelude* by starting at "Brother John." You can use the songs prior to "Brother John" as harmonization exercises where the students can compose and notate left hand intervals for those pieces. These pieces also provide the opportunity to introduce the concept of transposition. Blank staff paper is available at the end of this book.

Creative Transition: Use both books in tandem. Using *Keyboard Kickoff* and *Prelude* in parallel is extremely effective with beginners. The introduction of concepts overlaps seamlessly until you reach the halfway point of *Prelude* (at "Merrily We Roll Along"). At that point you should set *Prelude* aside and finish *Keyboard Kickoff*. Once finished with *Keyboard Kickoff* you can pick up where you left off in the *Prelude* book.

WHAT SHOULD I USE TO SUPPLEMENT? The Piano Pronto series offers a strong foundation of music fundamentals through a wide variety of pieces from different genres of music. While the series is comprehensive and designed to be used exclusively, I encourage teachers to seek out additional supplemental material for each individual student. The *Pronto Pizazz* books are great sources for supplemental materials. All of the solos stand alone, but have the added benefit of lush, contemporary teacher duet parts that will motivate and excite students of all ages. Additionally, I strongly recommend that you use the *Prelude: Teacher Duet Parts* book with your students. Playing duets is an ideal way to help reinforce rhythmic concepts early in the lesson process.

Just the Basics

The Music Alphabet
A B C D E F G

♪ *Practice saying the music alphabet backward a few times!*

Exploring the Keyboard

The piano keyboard is made up of black keys and white keys. The black keys are arranged in groups of twos and threes.

♪ *Circle a group of 2 black keys.*

♪ *Circle a group of 3 black keys.*

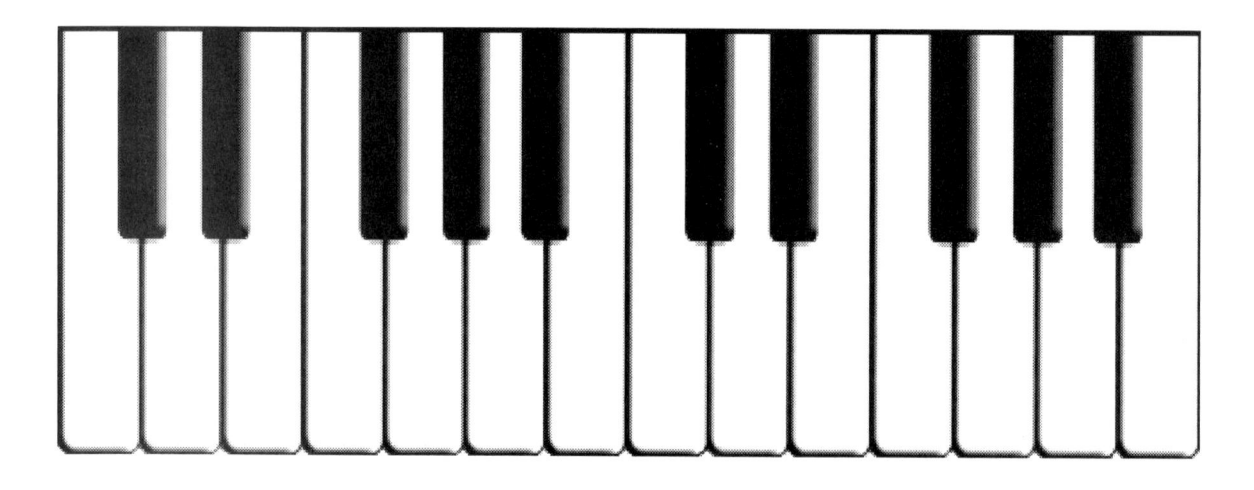

DOWN
(lower sounds)

Pitch = highness or lowness of a sound

UP
(higher sounds)

As we move DOWN
the piano
the alphabet goes
BACKWARD

As we move UP
the piano
the alphabet goes
FORWARD

Finding the "A"

To find "A" on the piano, locate a group of three black keys. "A" is the white key in between the 2nd and 3rd black keys.

♪ *Find the other "A" and label it on the keyboard below.*

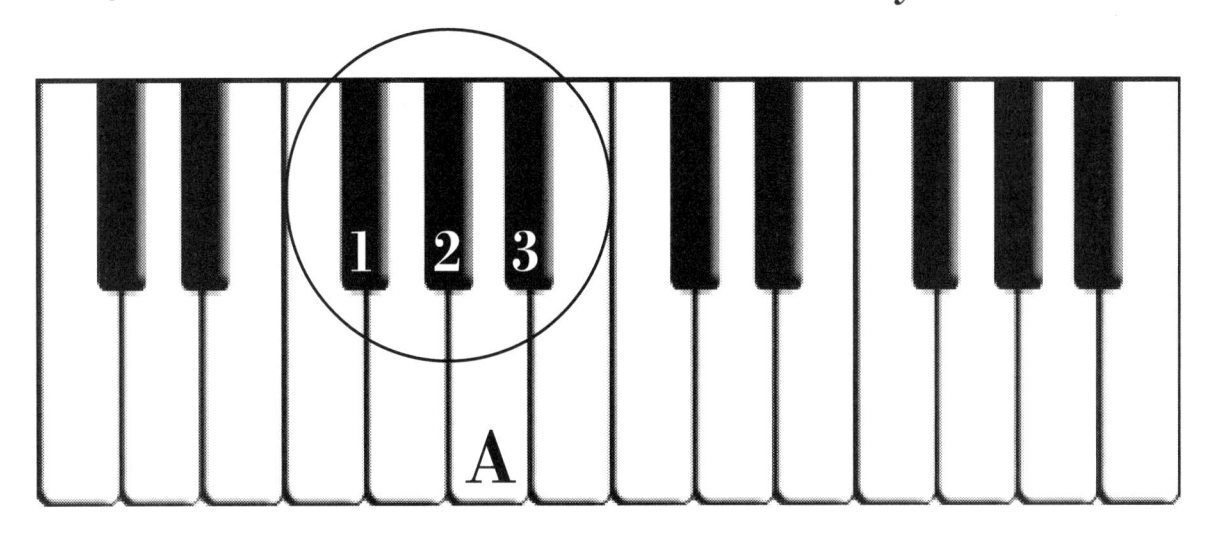

Now It's Your Turn

♪ *Label the "A's" on the keyboard below.*

♪ *Label the rest of the keys.*

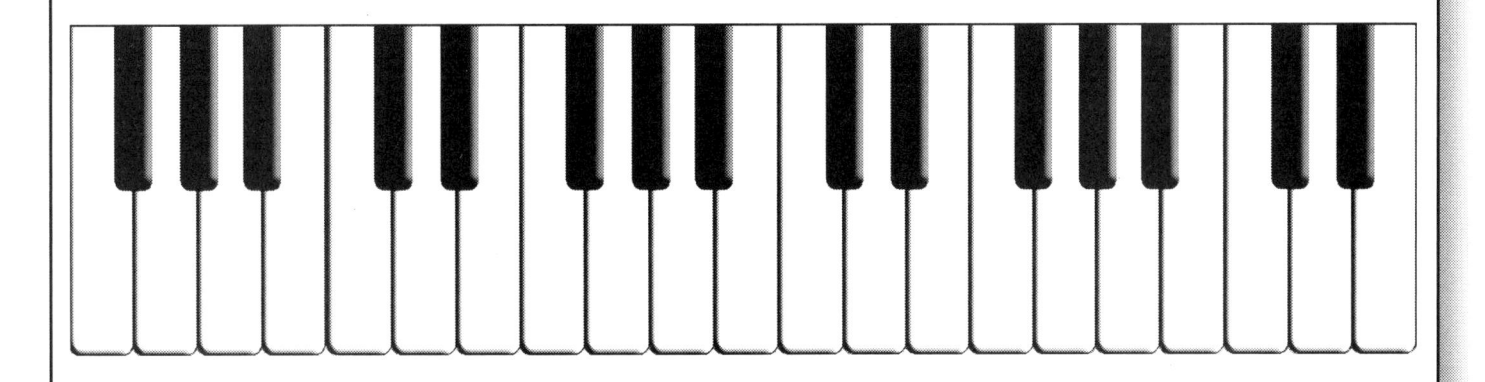

♪ *What is the HIGHEST key on your piano?* _____

♪ *What is the LOWEST key on your piano?* _____

Rhythm

Rhythm is made up of long sounds and short sounds. In order to write different rhythms we use notes. The way a note looks determines how long the note should be held down. Here are three types of notes you will encounter as you start playing:

♩ **Quarter Note** = 1 beat *(think: "hold" or "play")*

𝅗𝅥 **Half Note** = 2 beats *(think: "hold-it")*

𝅝 **Whole Note** = 4 beats *(think: "hold-this-long-note")*

Now It's Your Turn

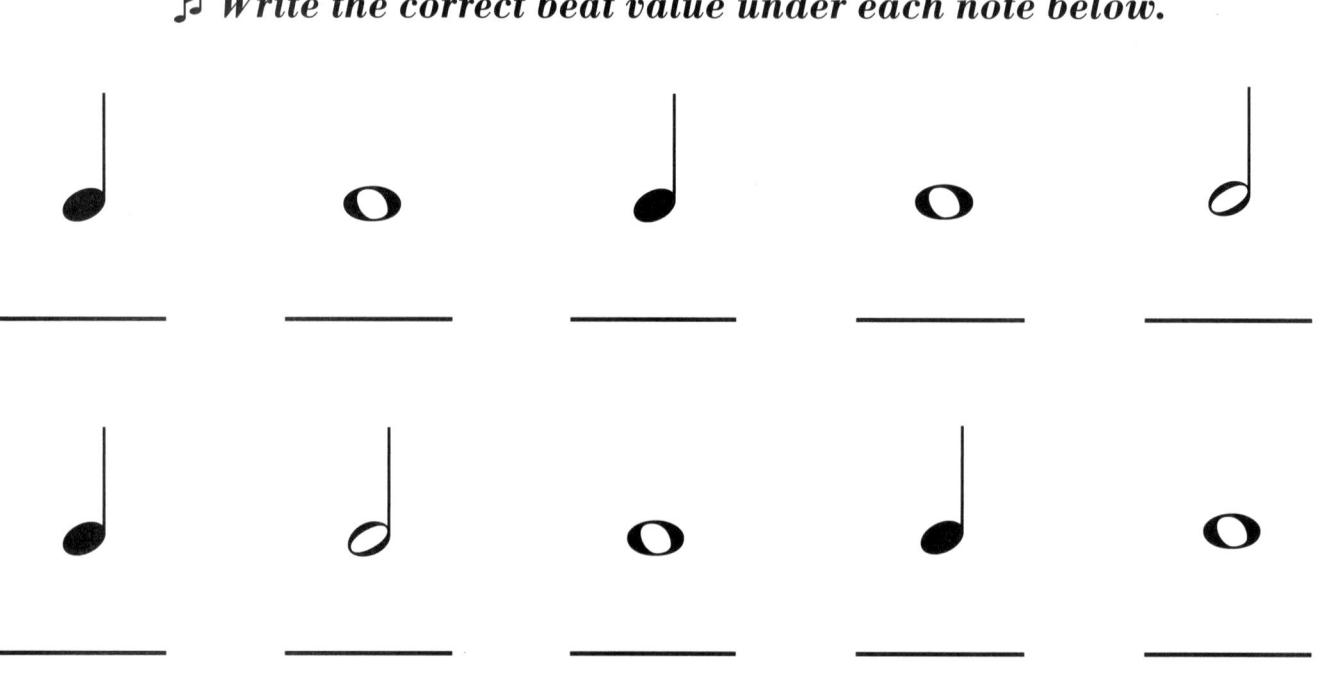

♪ *Write the correct beat value under each note below.*

___ ___ ___ ___ ___

___ ___ ___ ___ ___

The Grand Staff

Music is a language! To play the piano you read notes that are placed on the **grand staff** (pictured to the right). Just like words form sentences to tell stories, notes are placed on the grand staff to create songs.

Every key on the piano has its own unique location on this staff. The grand staff has two clefs: **treble clef** and **bass clef**.

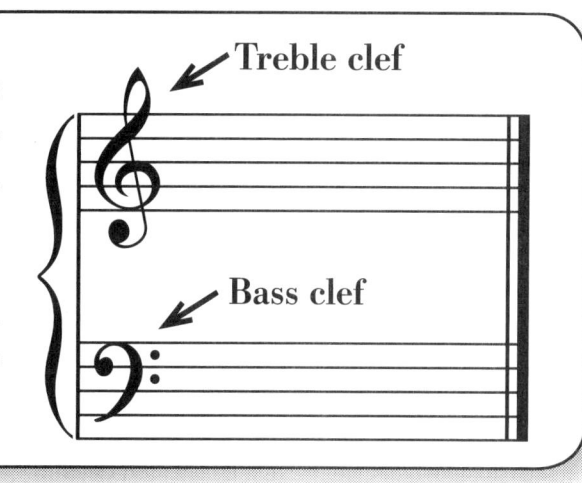

← Treble clef

← Bass clef

Note Parts

← stem
← head

← flag

← beam

Finding Middle C

Find the "C" closest to the middle of your piano. This is called **Middle C**. Let's take a look at what Middle C looks like when it is placed on the grand staff.

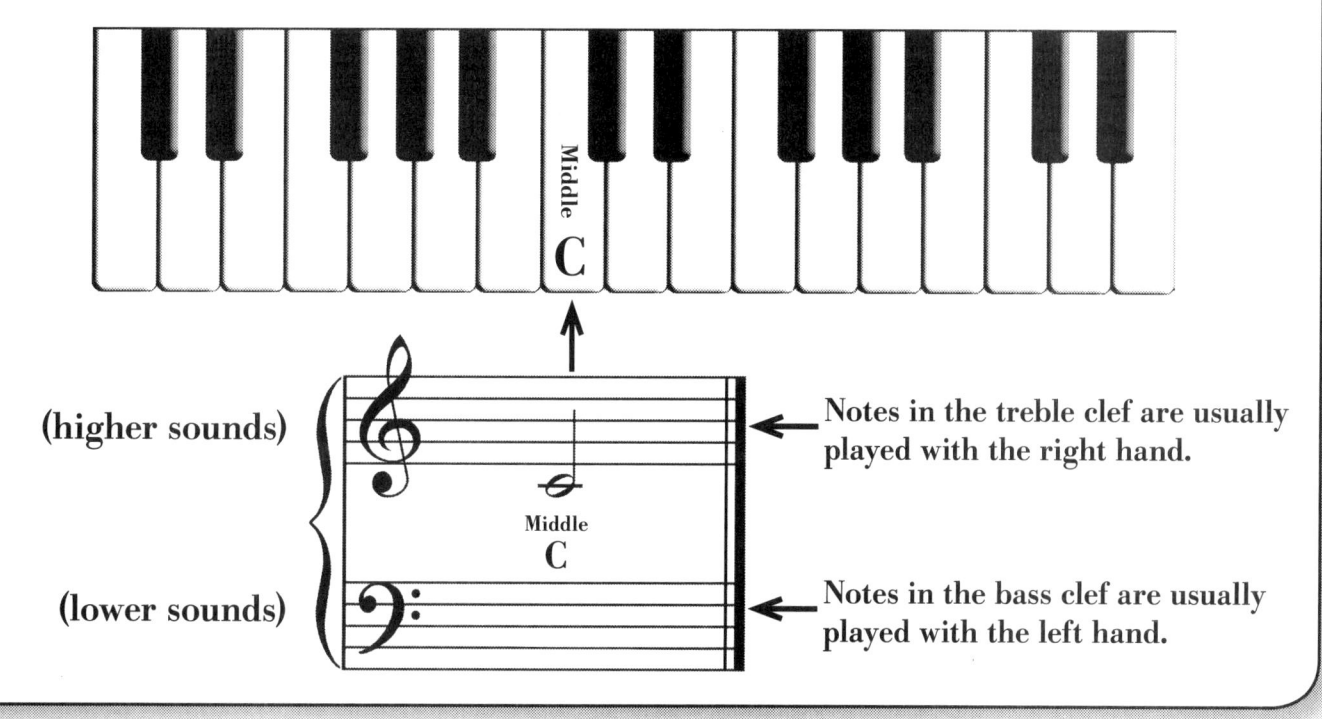

Middle C

(higher sounds) ← Notes in the treble clef are usually played with the right hand.

Middle C

(lower sounds) ← Notes in the bass clef are usually played with the left hand.

Measures & Barlines

Music is divided into **measures** (they look like boxes).
Measures are separated by **barlines**.

BARLINE

FINAL
BARLINE
end of the song

Time Signatures

Time signatures are placed at the beginning of each piece of music. The top number tells you how many beats are in each measure. In the following example, the **beat numbers** are written below each measure.

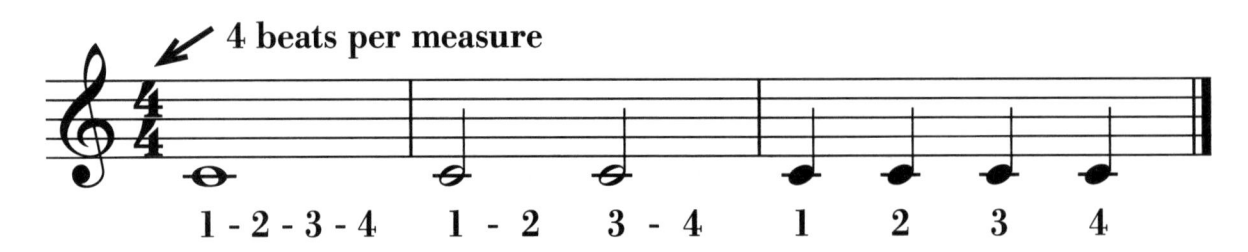

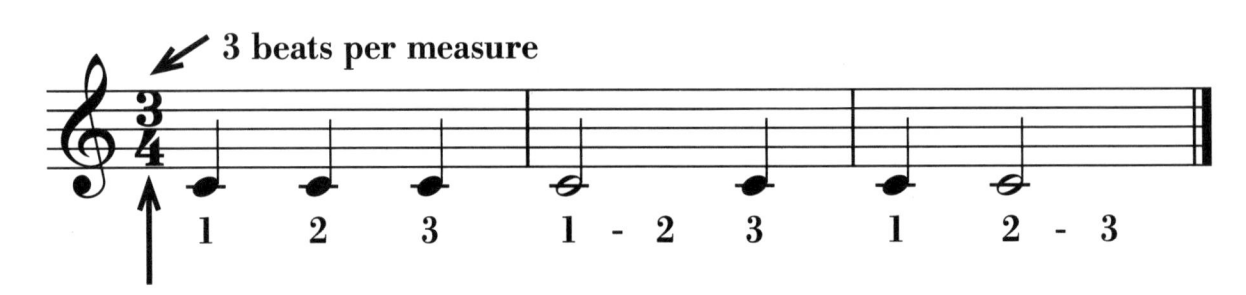

4 beats per measure

1 - 2 - 3 - 4   1 - 2   3 - 4   1   2   3   4

3 beats per measure

1   2   3   1 - 2   3   1   2 - 3

The bottom number of the **time signature** determines what **type of note** receives one beat. If there is a "4" on the bottom, it means that the **quarter note** receives one beat.

Finger Numbers

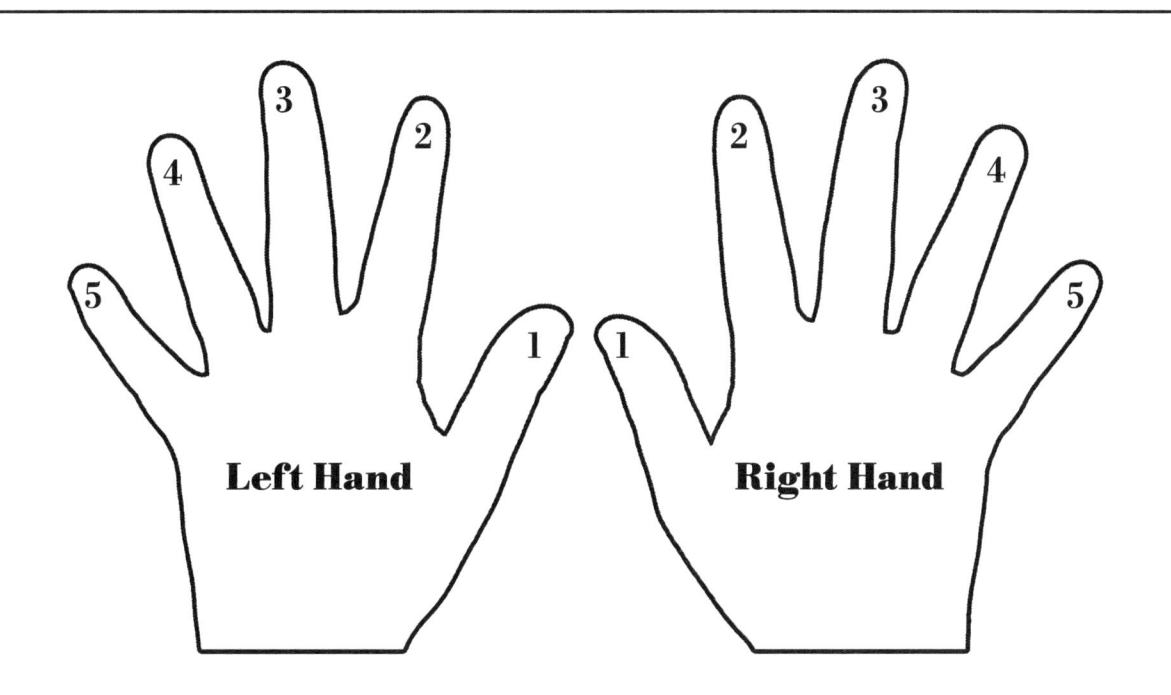

Left Hand   **Right Hand**

TIP: *You can think of left and right hands as "lower" (left) and "upper" (right).*

C Position (home base...for now)

In the beginning you will place your hands in **C Position**. You can think of it as your "home base," but only for a little while! As you progress you will use your note-reading skills and finger numbers to move all around the piano.

♪ *Look at the picture below and place your right hand in C Position.*

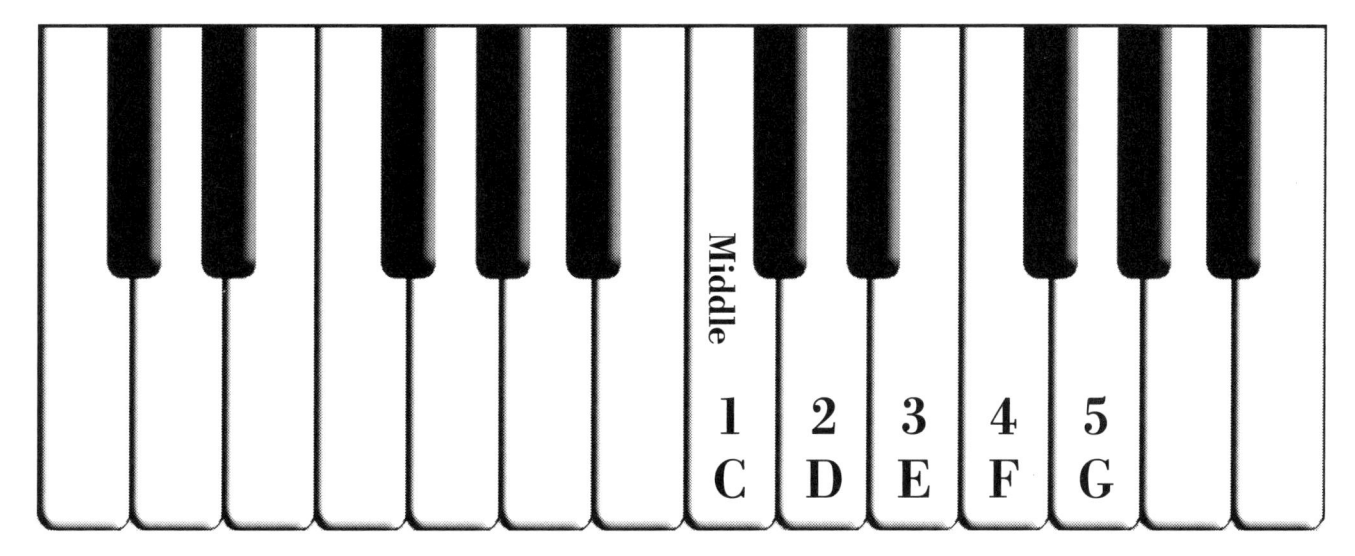

Middle

1 C   2 D   3 E   4 F   5 G

Place your right-hand fingers as shown above.

C Position on the Grand Staff

Look at the picture below to see how the notes of C Position look on the grand staff.

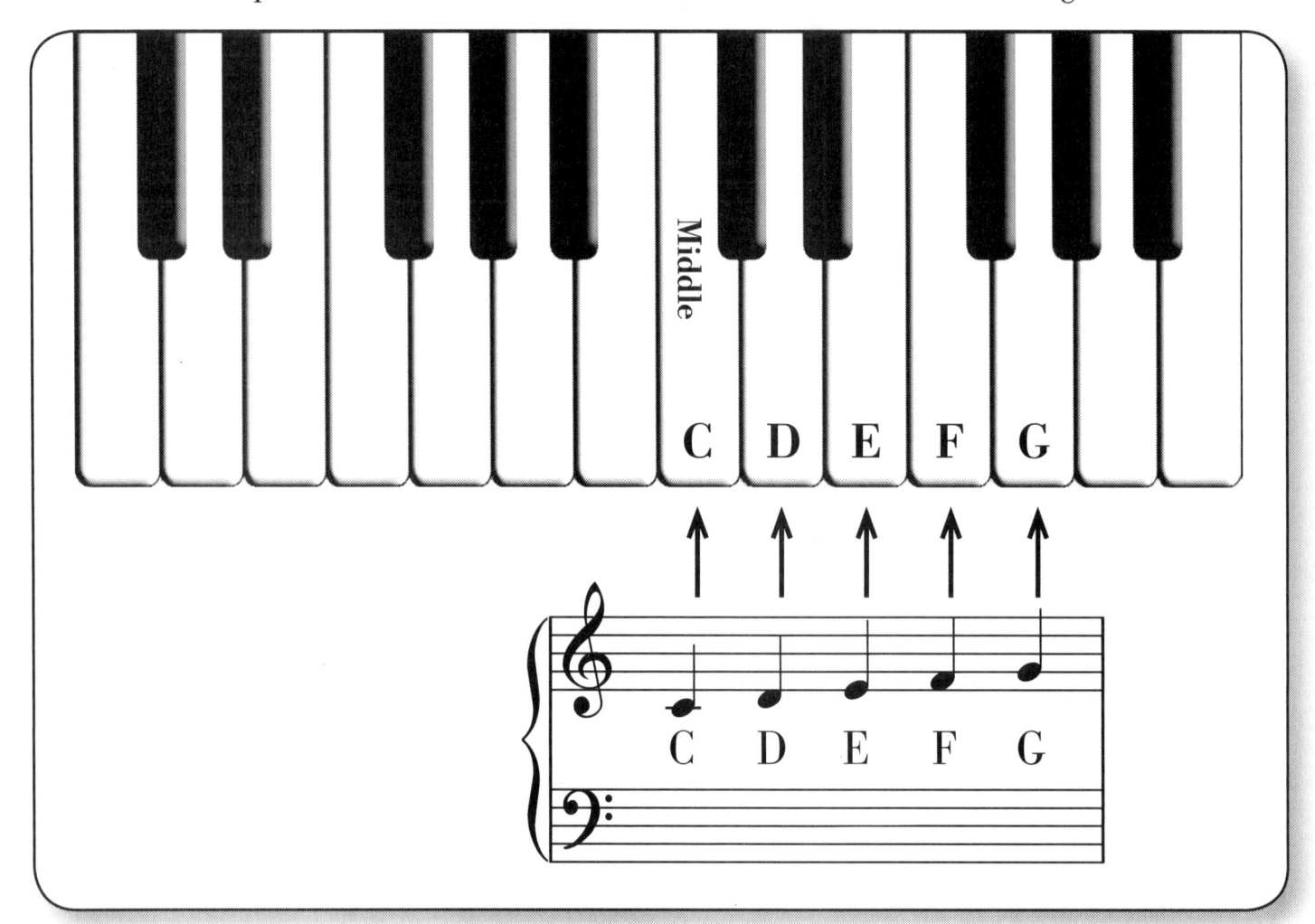

READY TO PLAY!

Here are some tips about how to sit properly at the piano:

♪ *Sit up tall toward the front edge of the bench with your feet flat on the floor. If your feet do not reach the floor it is a good idea use a footstool to support them.*

♪ *Place your right hand on the piano in C Position, keeping your fingers slightly curved, not flat. Your natural hand position at the piano should be the same as when you are standing up with your arms relaxed at the sides of your body.*

♪ *Keep your wrist even with the top of your hand. Don't let it drop and rest on the piano as this makes it difficult to use your fingers independently.*

♪ *Take a deep breath, relax, and most importantly, have fun!*

Before you begin:

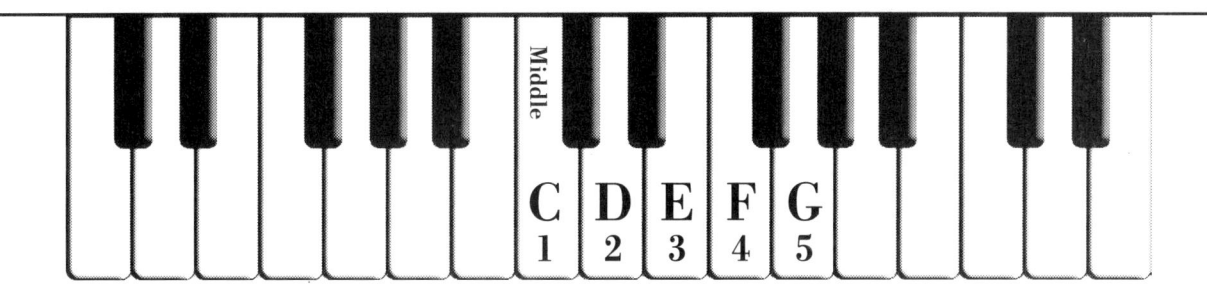

♪ Circle the **whole notes** in the next piece. How many did you find? _____

♪ The other notes in the song are:

half notes   *or*   **quarter notes**

1. My First Steps

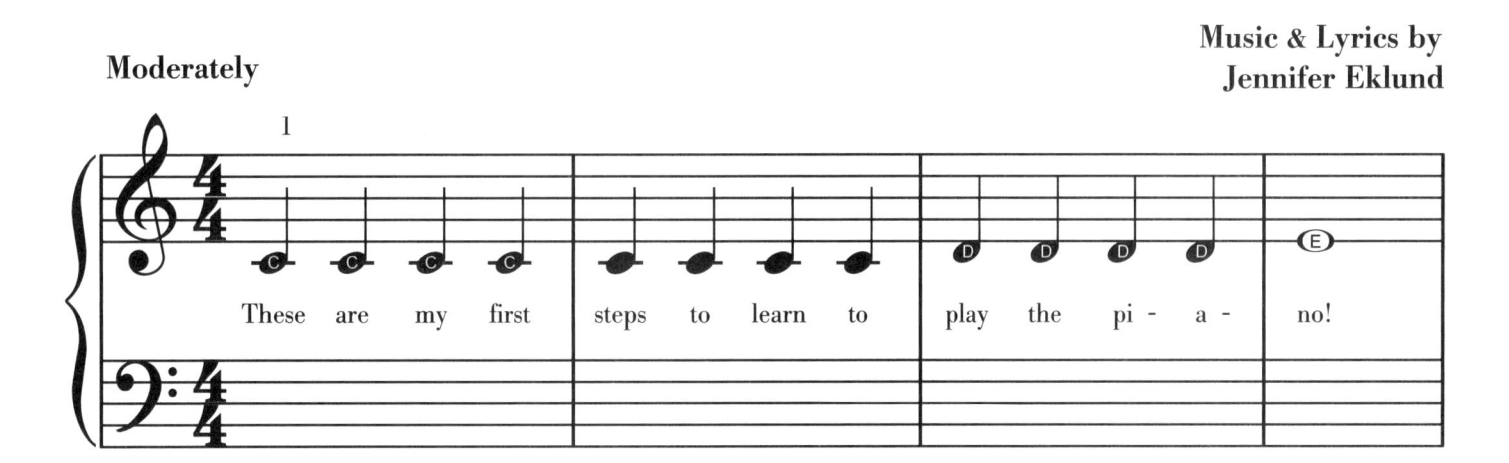

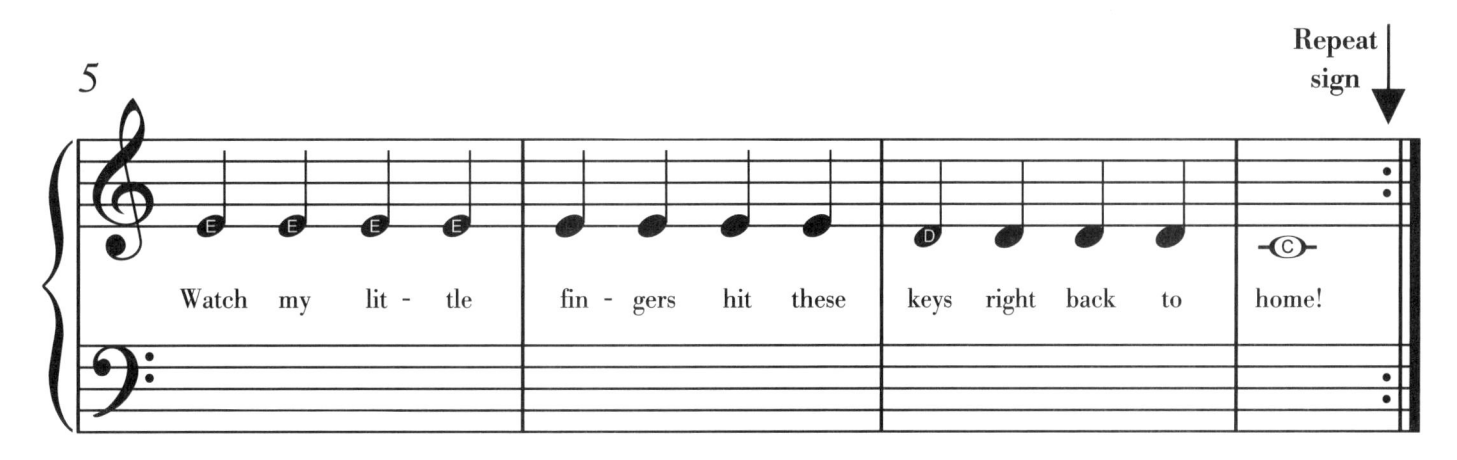

Music & Lyrics by
Jennifer Eklund

Moderately

These are my first | steps to learn to | play the pi - a - | no!

Watch my lit - tle | fin - gers hit these | keys right back to | home!

Repeat sign

Copyright © 2015 Piano Pronto Publishing, Inc.
All Rights Reserved | PianoPronto.com

Before you begin:

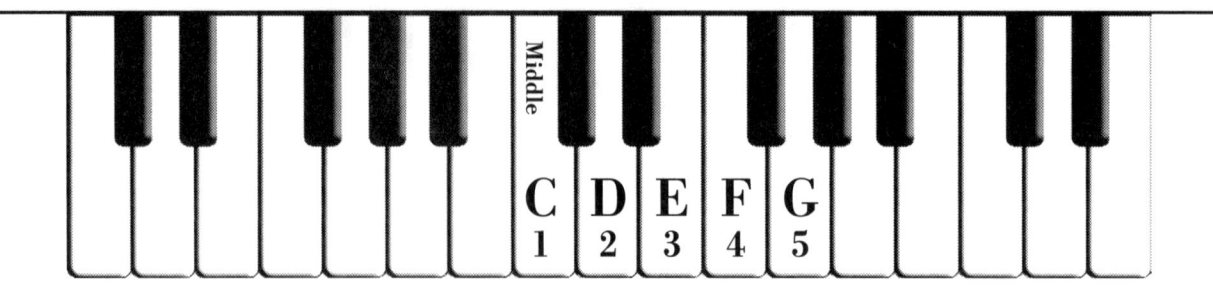

♪ Circle the **half notes**. How many did you find? _____

♪ Put a box around the **whole notes**. How many did you find? _____

♪ Write in the **beat numbers** under these notes.

2. Song for the Moon

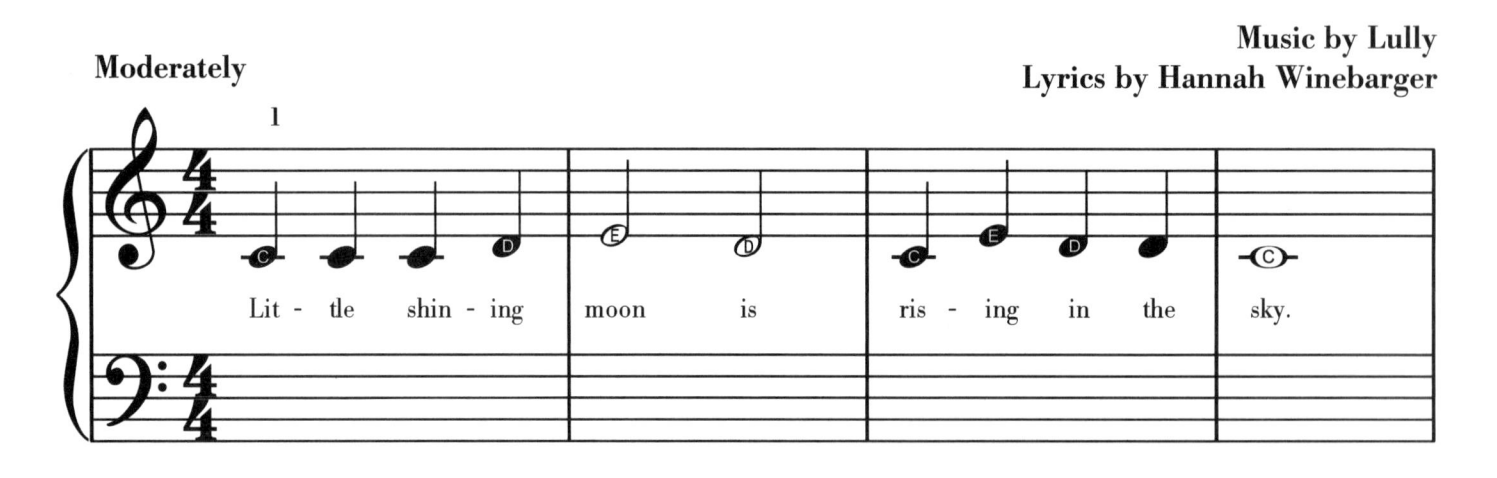

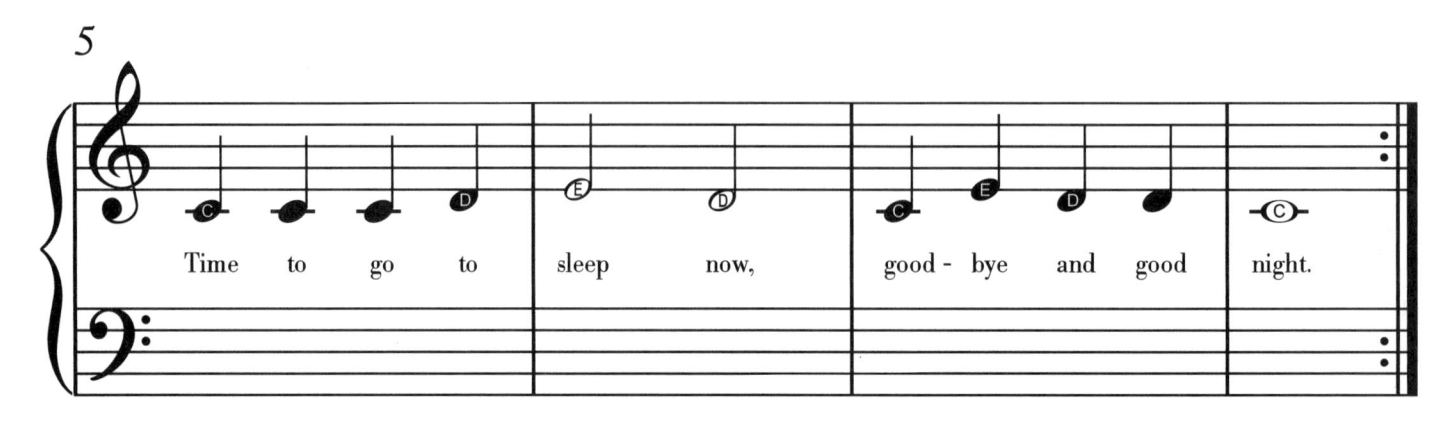

Music by Lully
Lyrics by Hannah Winebarger

Moderately

Lit - tle shin - ing moon is ris - ing in the sky.

Time to go to sleep now, good - bye and good night.

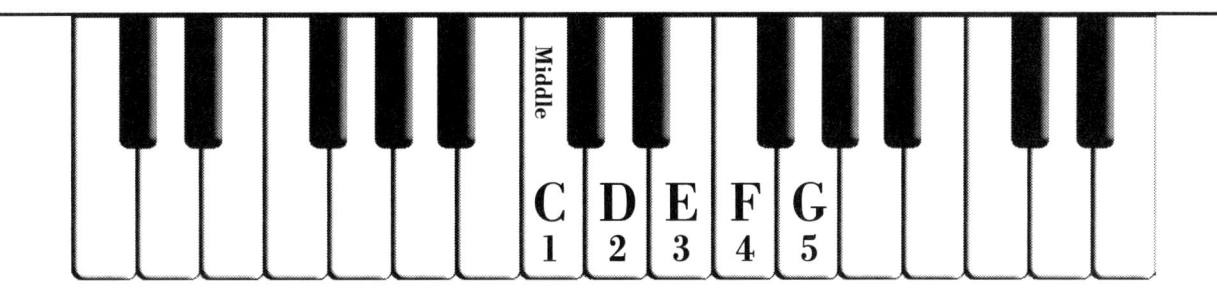

Before you begin:

♪ Circle the **time signature**.

♪ How many **beats** are found in each **measure**? **4** *or* 8

♪ This song begins with the note _____ played by finger number _____.

3. Mary Had a Little Lamb

Moderately Traditional

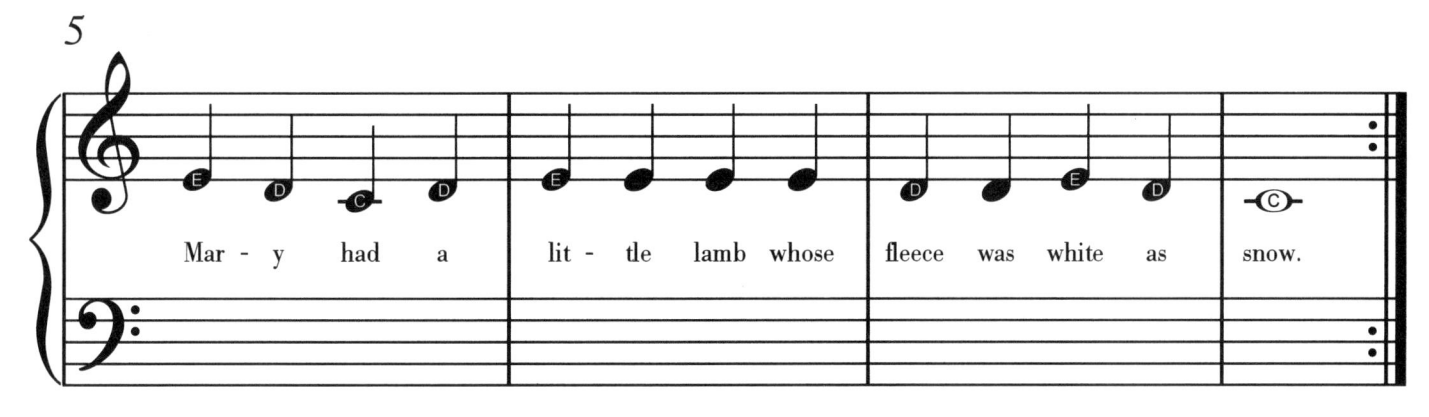

Mar-y had a lit-tle lamb, lit-tle lamb, lit-tle lamb.

Mar-y had a lit-tle lamb whose fleece was white as snow.

Copyright © 2015 Piano Pronto Publishing, Inc.
All Rights Reserved | PianoPronto.com

Before you begin:

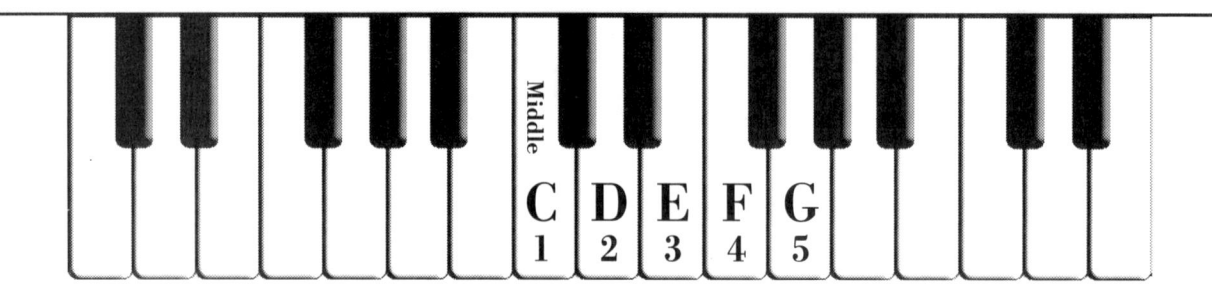

- ♪ **F** and **G** are used in this song. Find and circle these notes.

- ♪ How many **beats** are in each **measure**? _____

- ♪ This song begins with the note _____ played by finger number _____.

4. My Piano Song

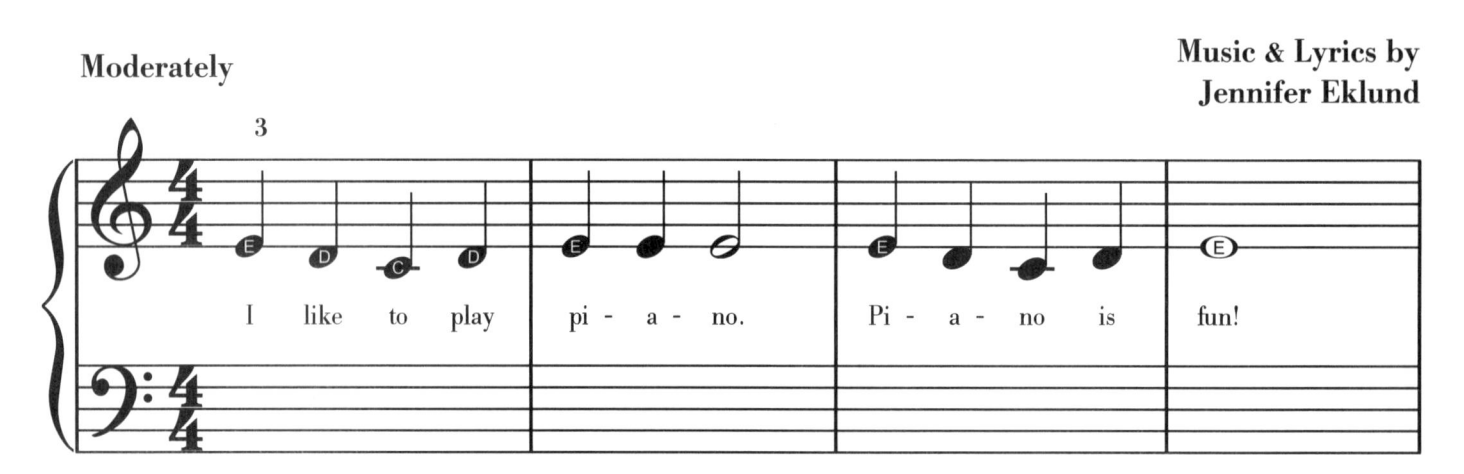

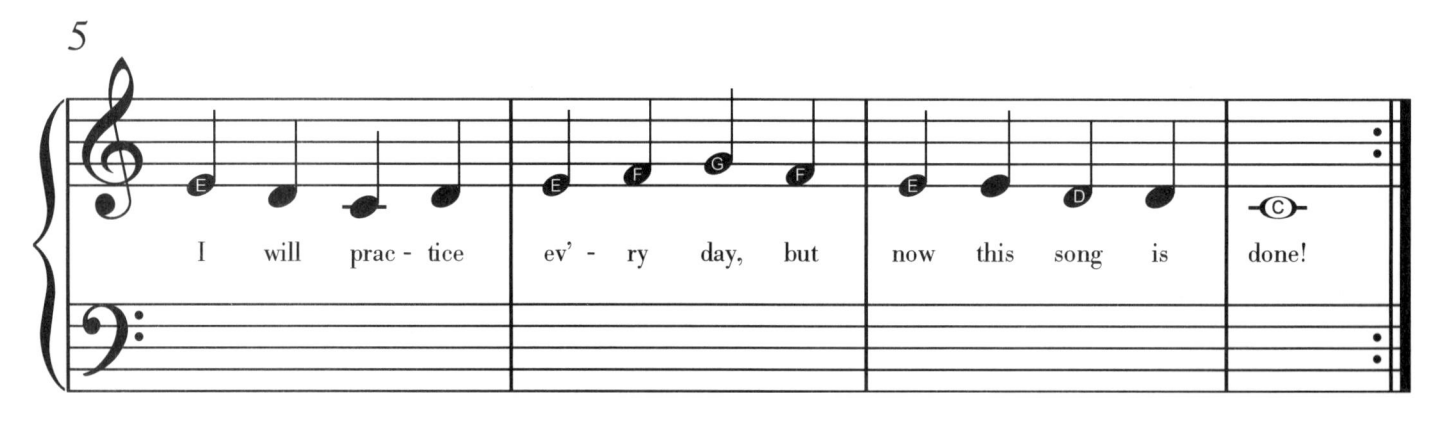

Moderately

Music & Lyrics by
Jennifer Eklund

Before you begin:

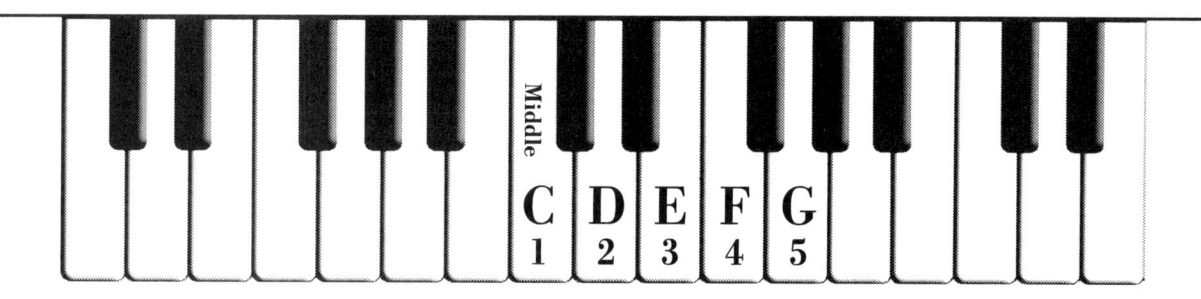

♪ Circle the **time signature**.

♪ How many **beats** are in each **measure**? _____

♪ This song begins with the note _____ played by finger number _____.

5. Good King What's-His-Face

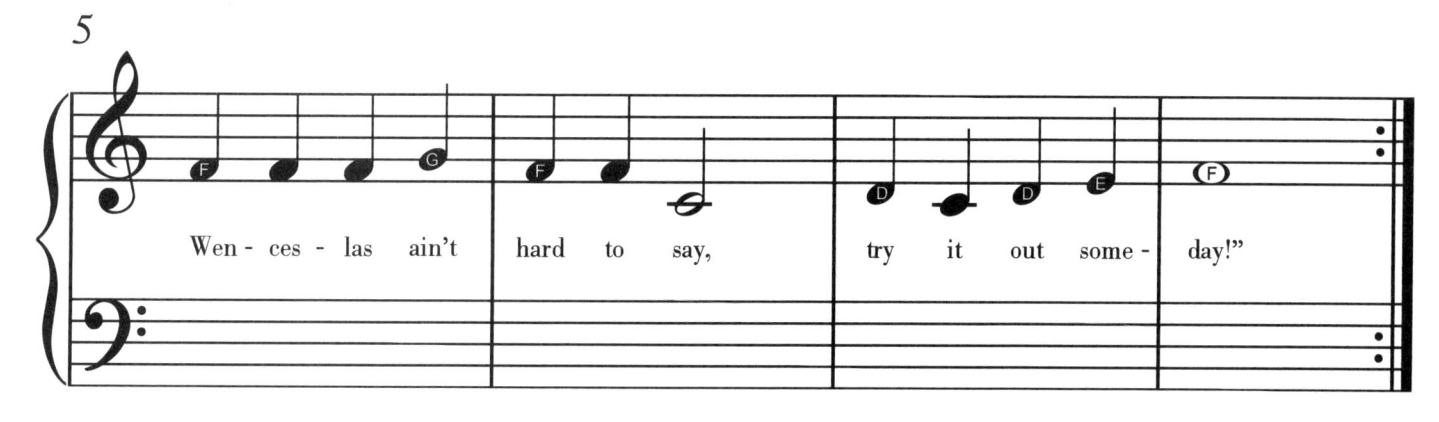

Moderately

Traditional
Lyrics by Jennifer Eklund

Good King What's-His-Face might say, "You should learn my real name!

Wen - ces - las ain't hard to say, try it out some - day!"

New Note

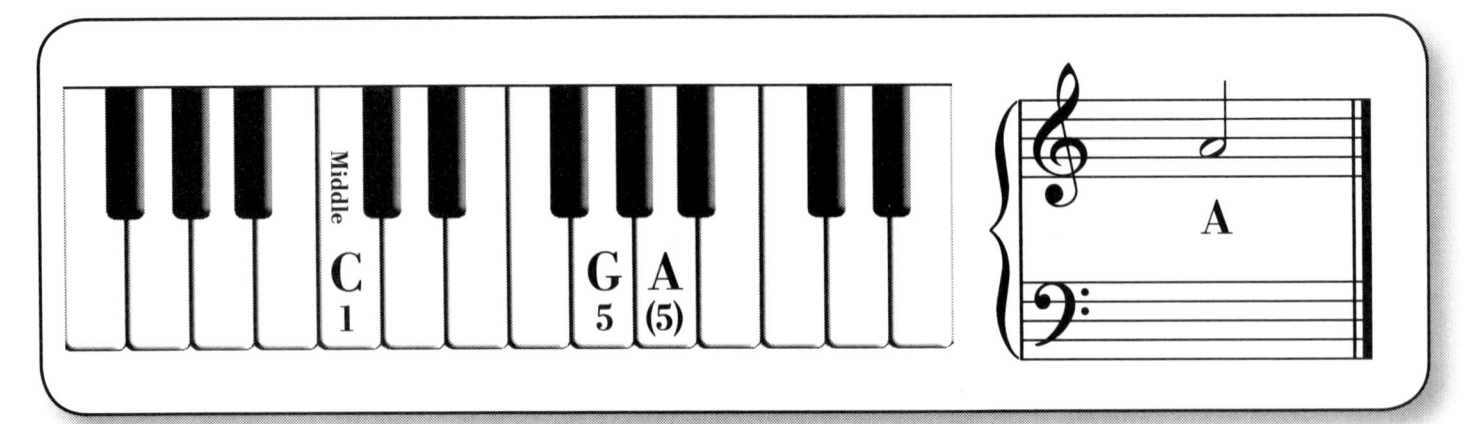

6. Pronto Prep

♪ *Play the examples to help prepare for* "Twinkle, Twinkle, Little Star."

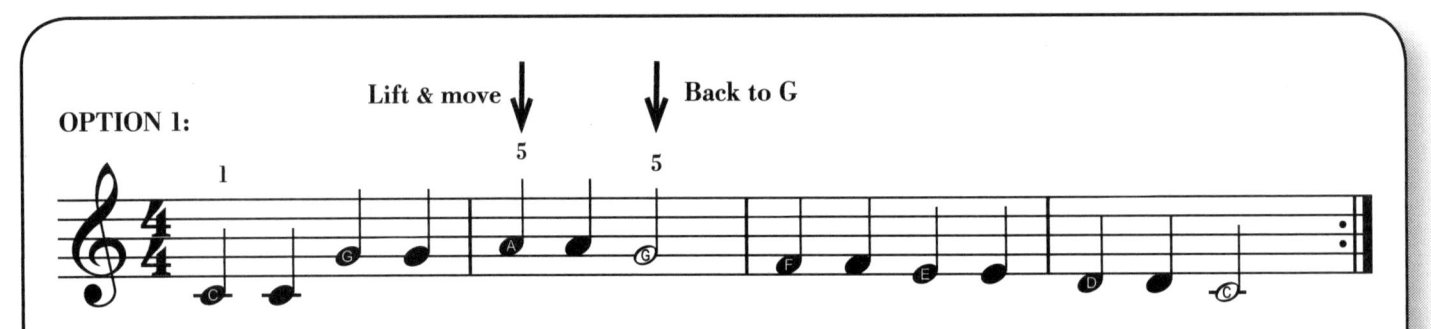

OPTION 1:

Lift & move ↓   Back to G ↓

ALTERNATIVE FINGERINGS

Finger numbers tell you where to place your hand, but often more than one fingering is possible. Choosing comfortable fingerings is an important part of learning new music. Try the alternative fingerings below and decide which is the best fit.

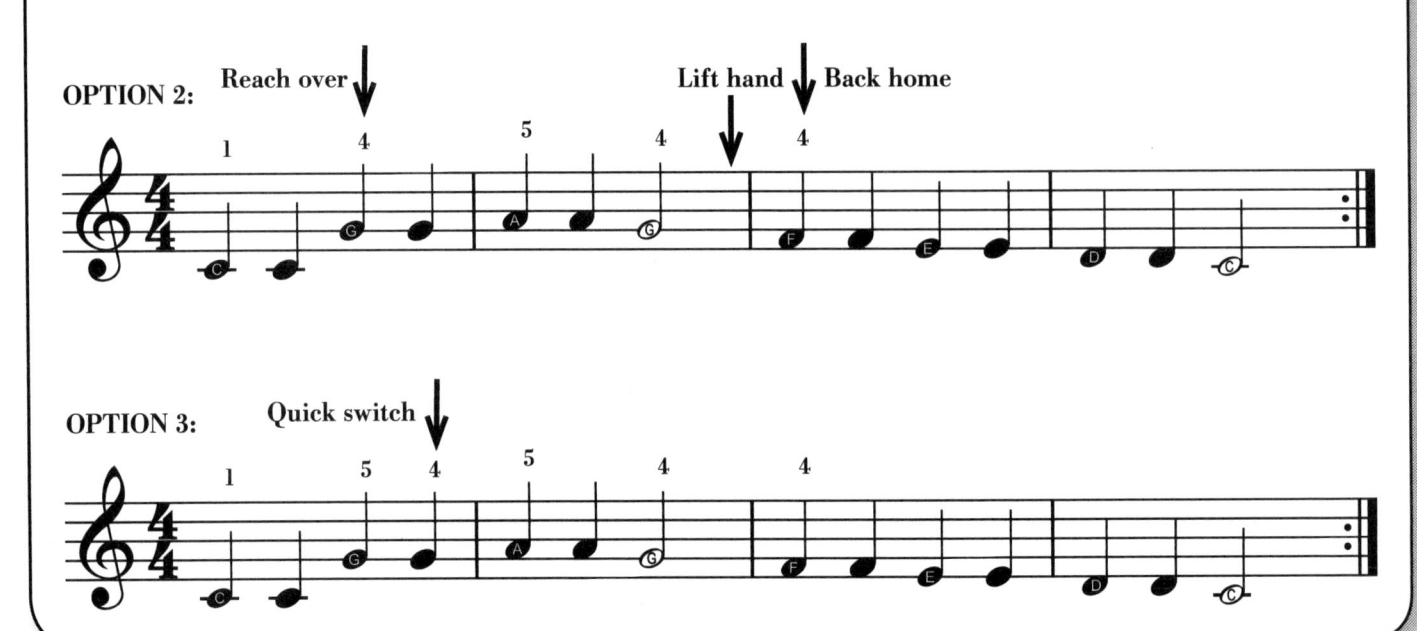

OPTION 2:

Reach over ↓   Lift hand ↓ Back home ↓

OPTION 3:

Quick switch ↓

16

> **Before you begin:**
>
> ♪ Which fingering option did you decide to use? _____
>
> ♪ Write in the fingerings you chose in the music below.

6. Twinkle, Twinkle, Little Star

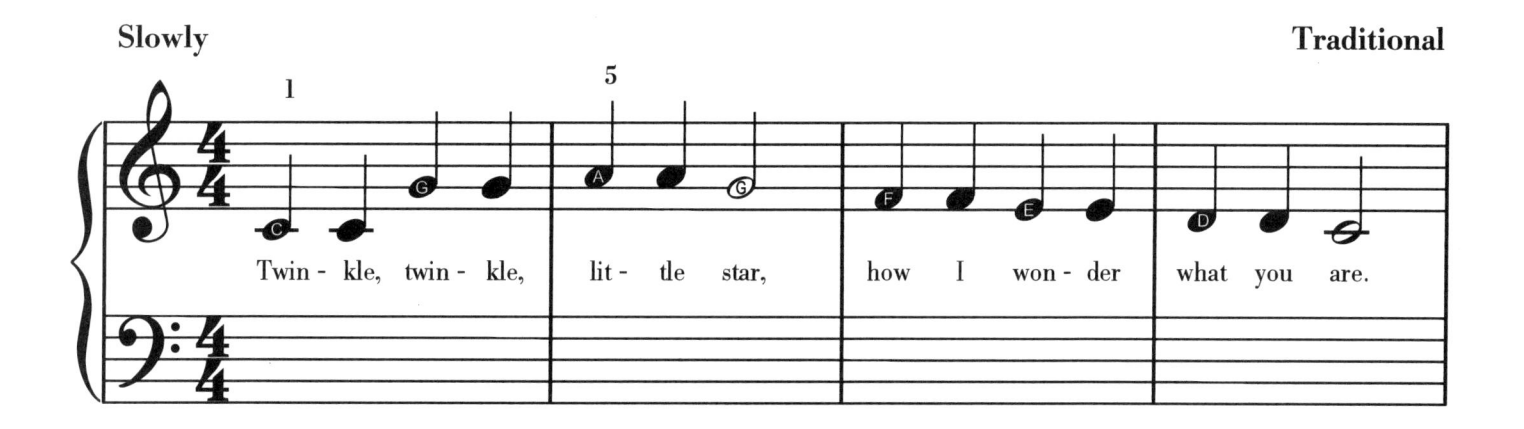

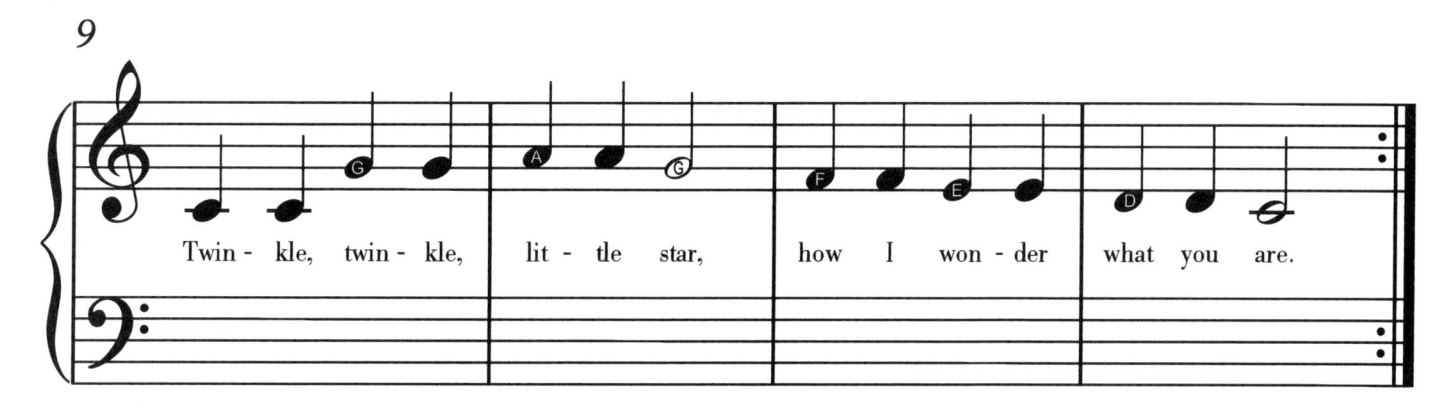

Slowly   **Traditional**

Twin - kle, twin - kle, lit - tle star, how I won - der what you are.

Up a - bove the world so high, like a dia - mond in the sky.

Twin - kle, twin - kle, lit - tle star, how I won - der what you are.

Copyright © 2015 Piano Pronto Publishing, Inc.
All Rights Reserved | PianoPronto.com

New Rhythm

𝅗𝅥. Dotted half note = 3 beats

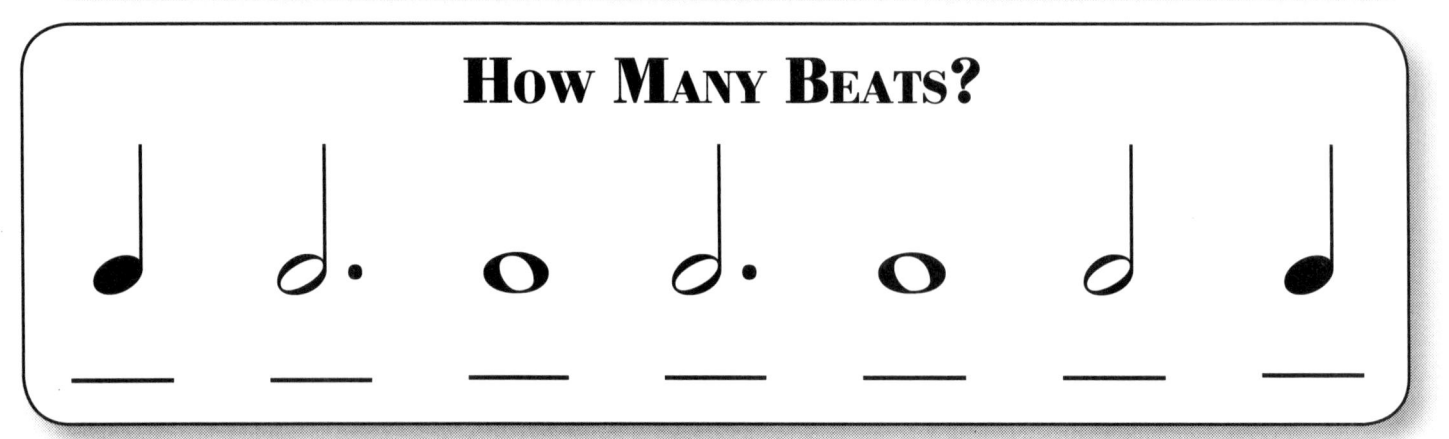

How Many Beats?

7. Pronto Prep

♪ *Play the examples to help prepare for "Farmer in the Dell."*

OPTION 1:

Alternative Fingering

OPTION 2:

Before you begin:

♪ *Write in the fingerings you chose in the music before you play.*

7. Farmer in the Dell

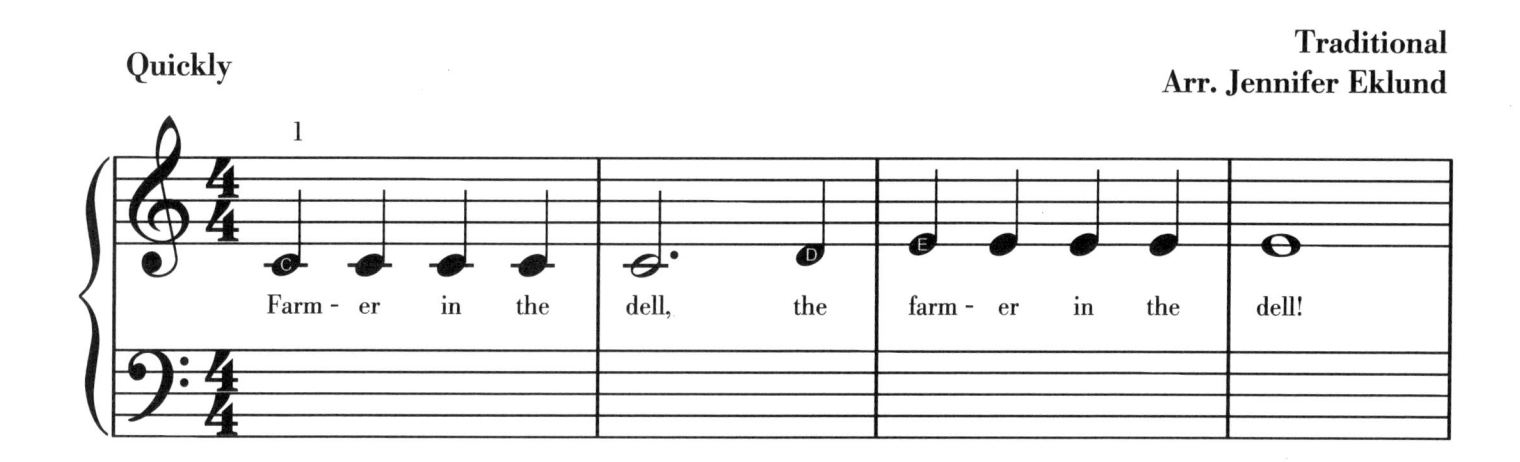

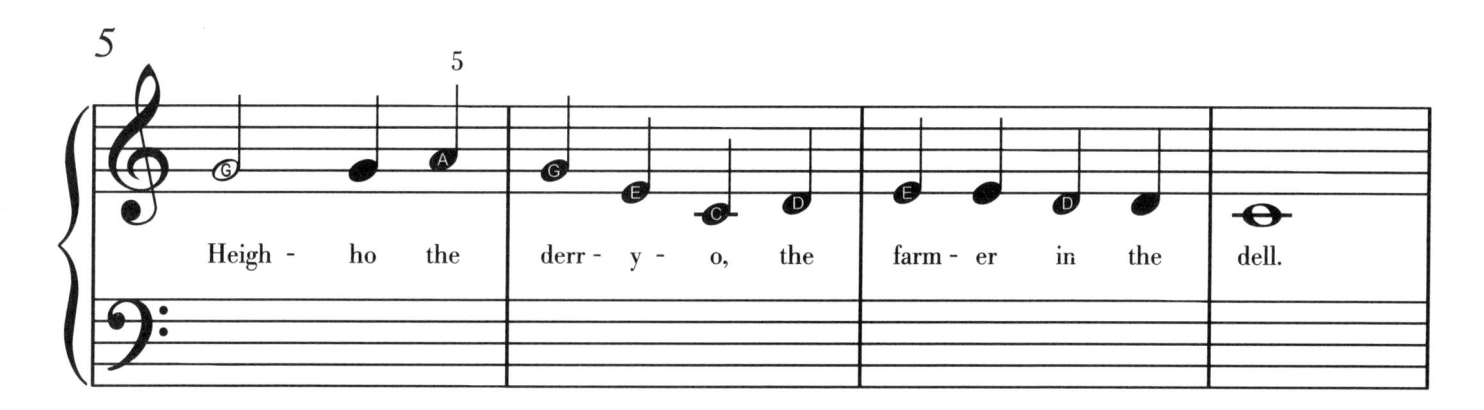

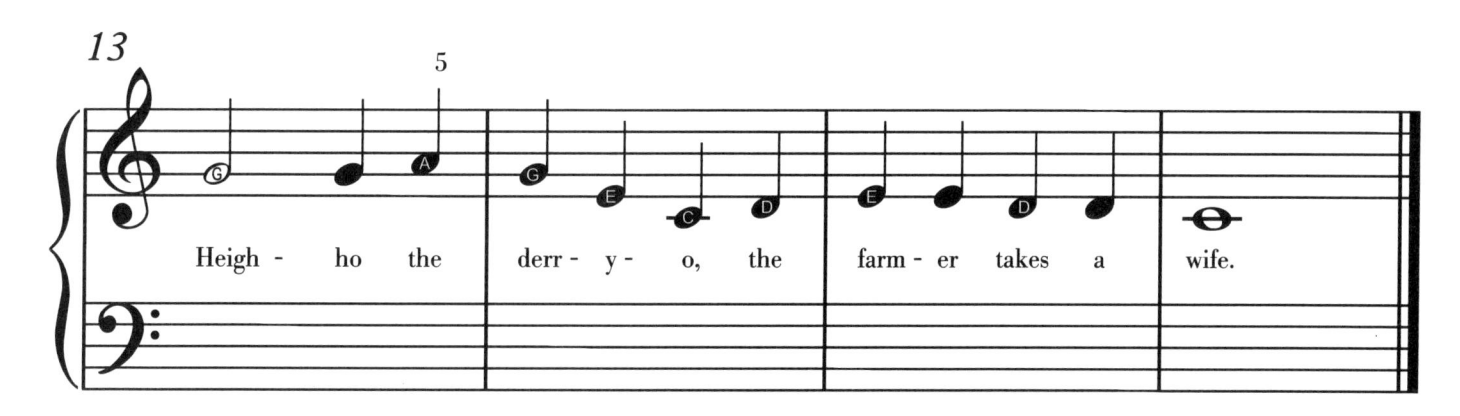

Traditional
Arr. Jennifer Eklund

Quickly

New Rhythm

♪ eighth note = ½ beat

When 2 eighth notes are placed together in pairs they look like this:

2 eighth notes = 1 beat

Now It's Your Turn

♪ *Play the following line of C's to practice eighth notes. Say the words as you play.*

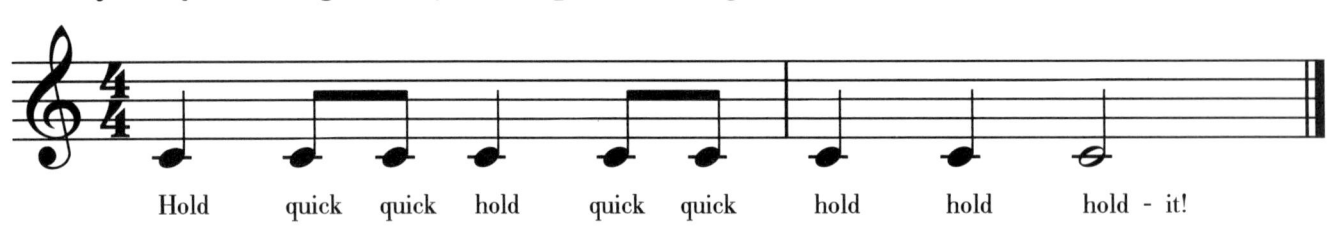

Hold quick quick hold quick quick hold hold hold - it!

♪ *Now try the same line counting the beat numbers instead of using words.*

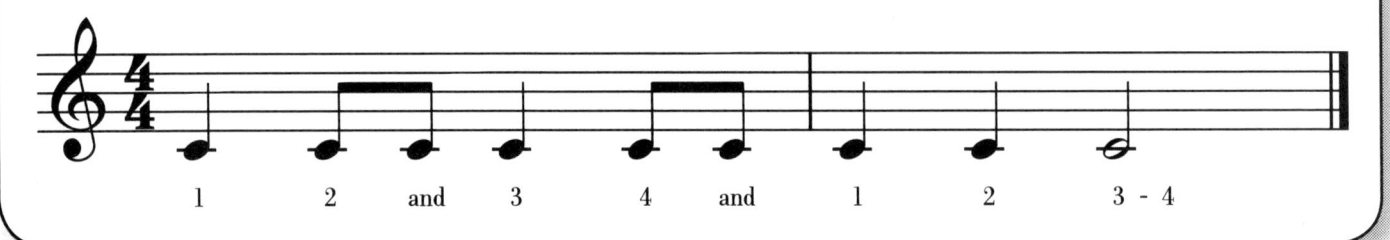

1 2 and 3 4 and 1 2 3 - 4

8. Pronto Prep

♪ *Play the example to help prepare for "Jingle Bells." Sing the lyrics.*

Oh what fun it is to ride in a one horse o - pen sleigh, hey!

8. Jingle Bells

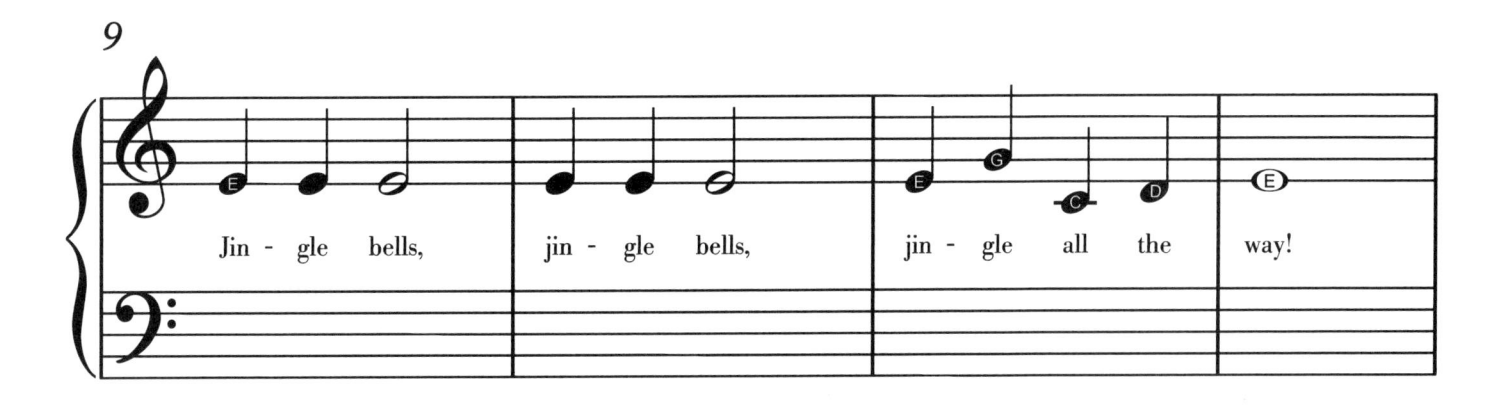

James Pierpont
Arr. Jennifer Eklund

Joyfully

More about the Grand Staff

It's time to start reading music without the help of letter names. Let's look more closely at the **grand staff** and how it is put together.

LINES & SPACES

The grand staff has **5 lines** and **4 spaces** in the treble and bass clefs.

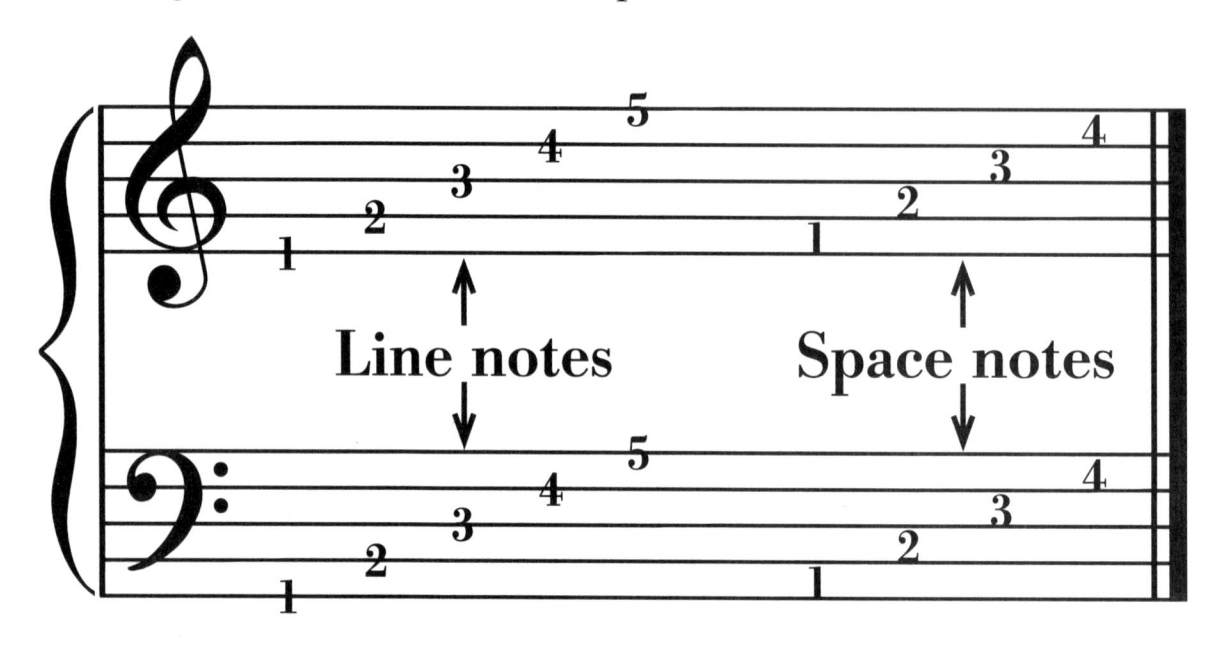

Line notes ↕   Space notes ↕

NOW IT'S YOUR TURN

Notes are placed ON A LINE or IN A SPACE.

C D E F G

♪ Which notes are **on a line**? _____

♪ Which notes are **in a space**? _____

9. Pronto Prep

♪ *Play the example below to help prepare for "Sweetly Sings the Donkey."*

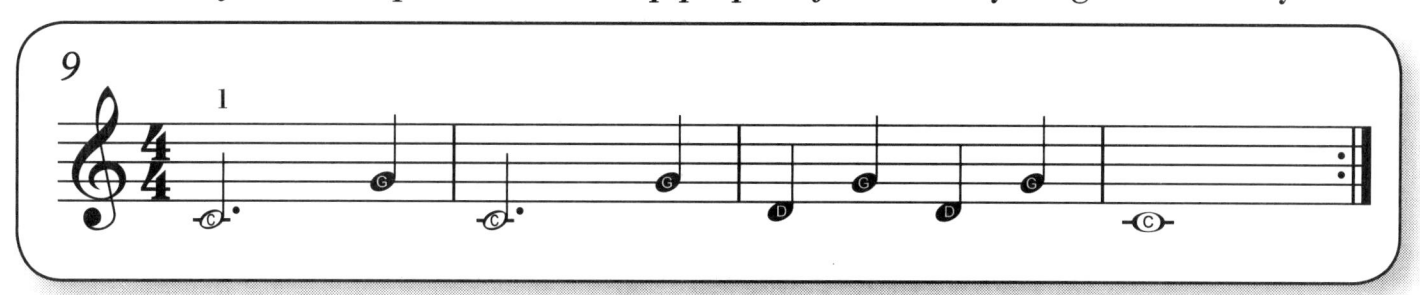

9. Sweetly Sings the Donkey

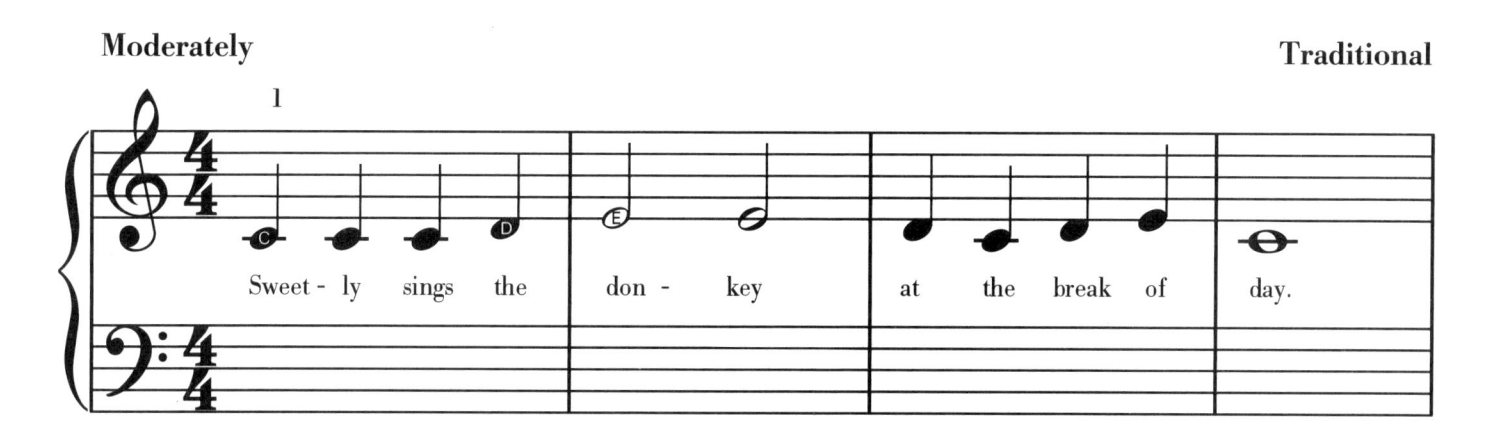

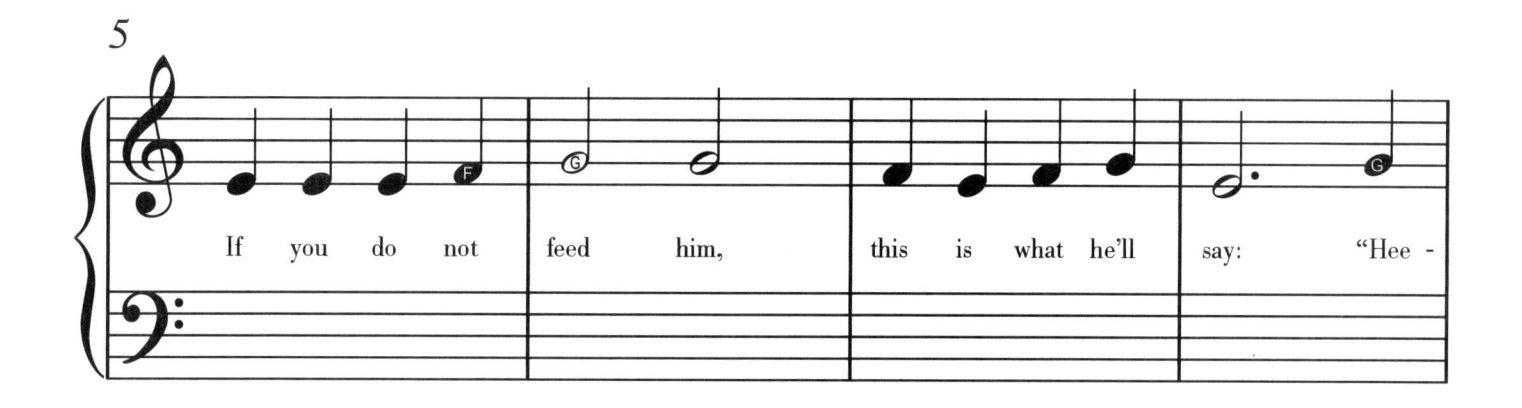

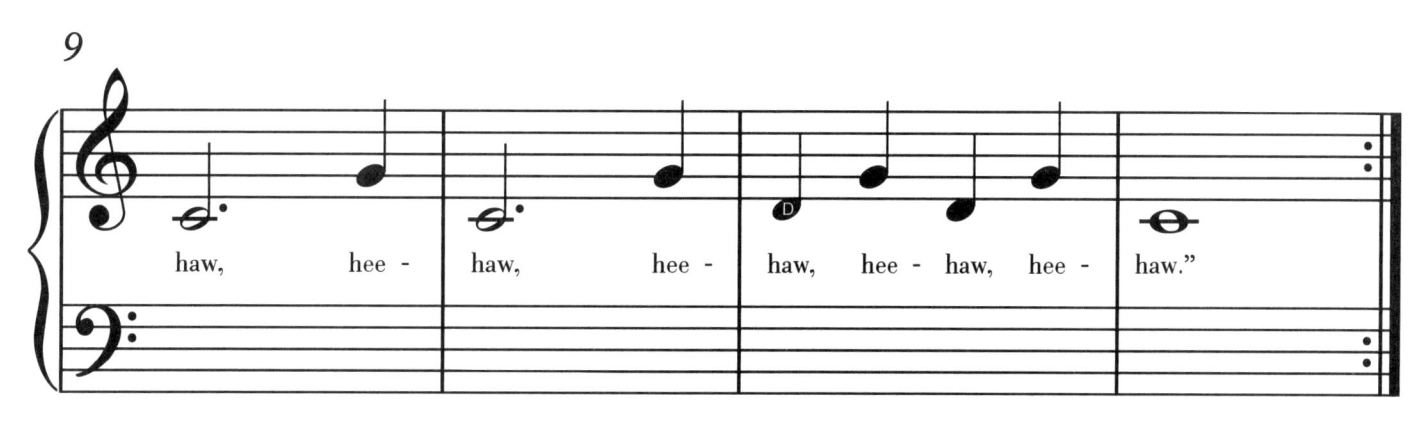

Moderately　　　　　　　　　　　　　　　　　　　　　　　　　　Traditional

Sweet - ly sings the don - key at the break of day.
If you do not feed him, this is what he'll say: "Hee -
haw, hee - haw, hee - haw, hee - haw, hee - haw."

Copyright © 2015 Piano Pronto Publishing, Inc.
All Rights Reserved | PianoPronto.com

C Position with Both Hands

The next piece uses a note in the bass clef, which means it is time to use the left hand! Look at the picture below to find out where to put the left hand fingers on the piano.

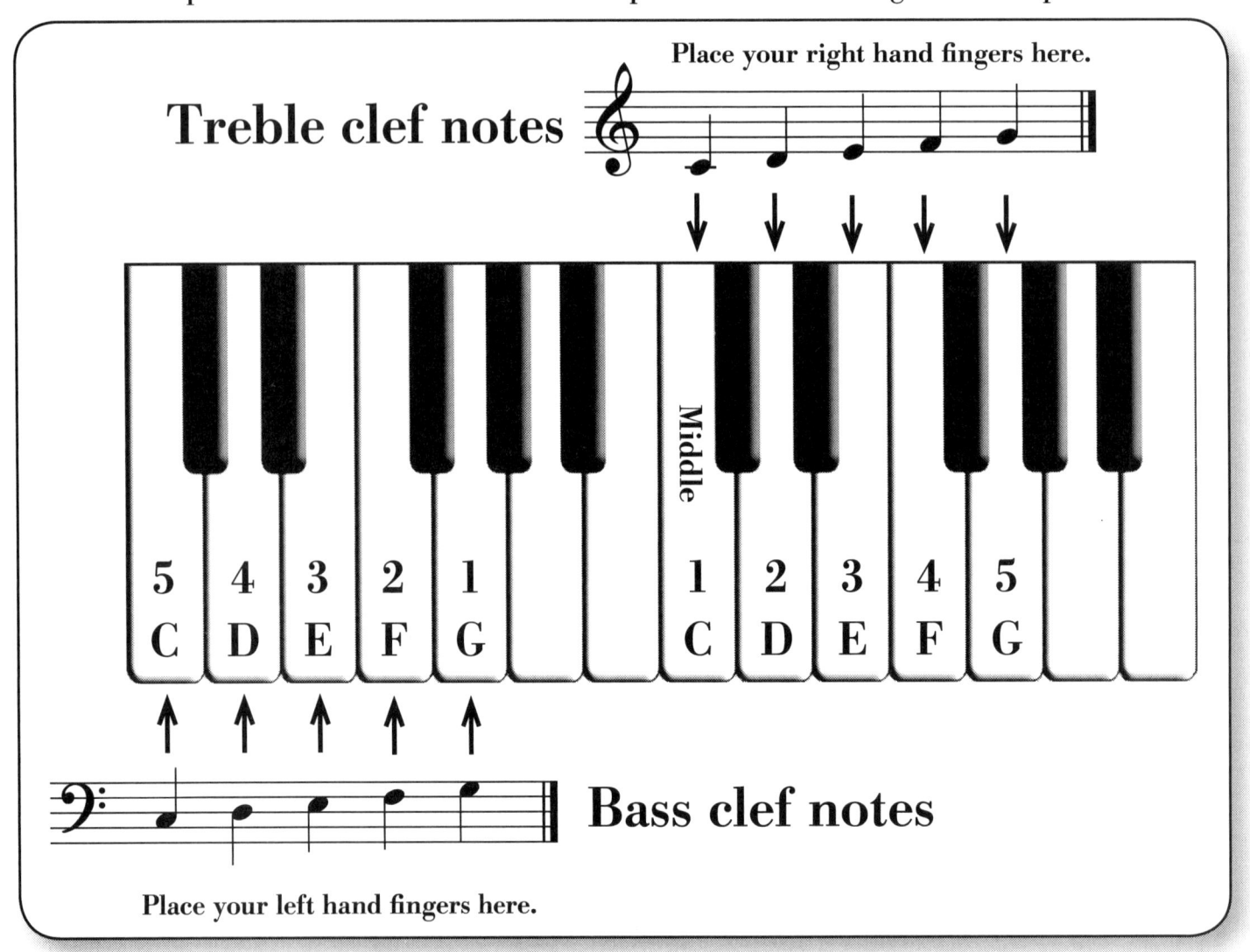

Place your right hand fingers here.

Treble clef notes

Bass clef notes

Place your left hand fingers here.

10. Pronto Prep

♪ *Play the example below to help prepare for "Ode to Joy."*

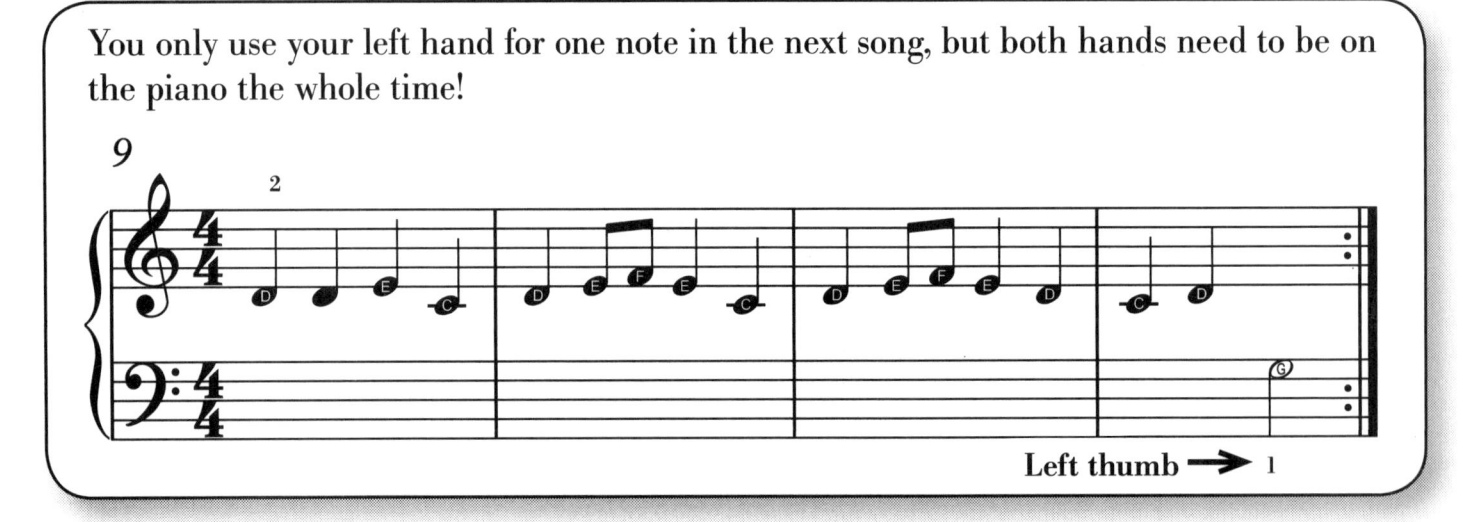

You only use your left hand for one note in the next song, but both hands need to be on the piano the whole time!

Left thumb → 1

10. Ode to Joy

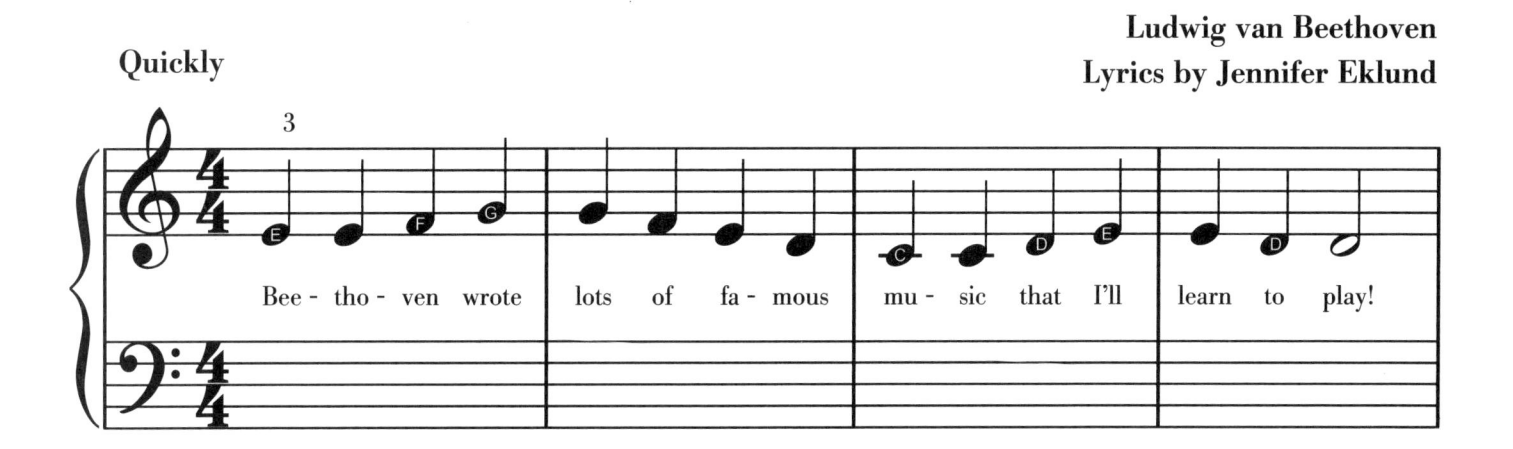

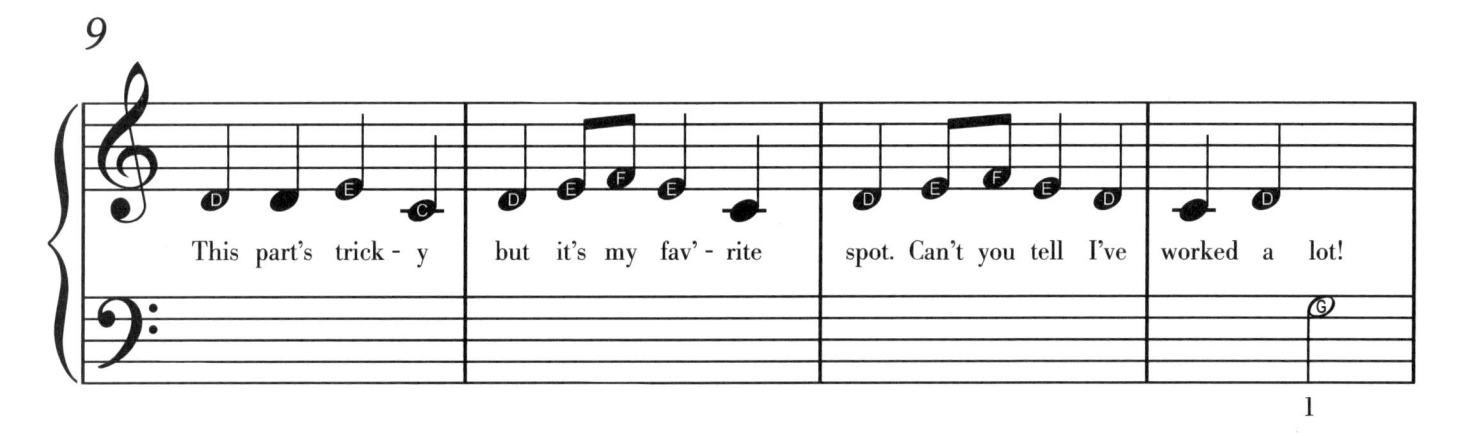

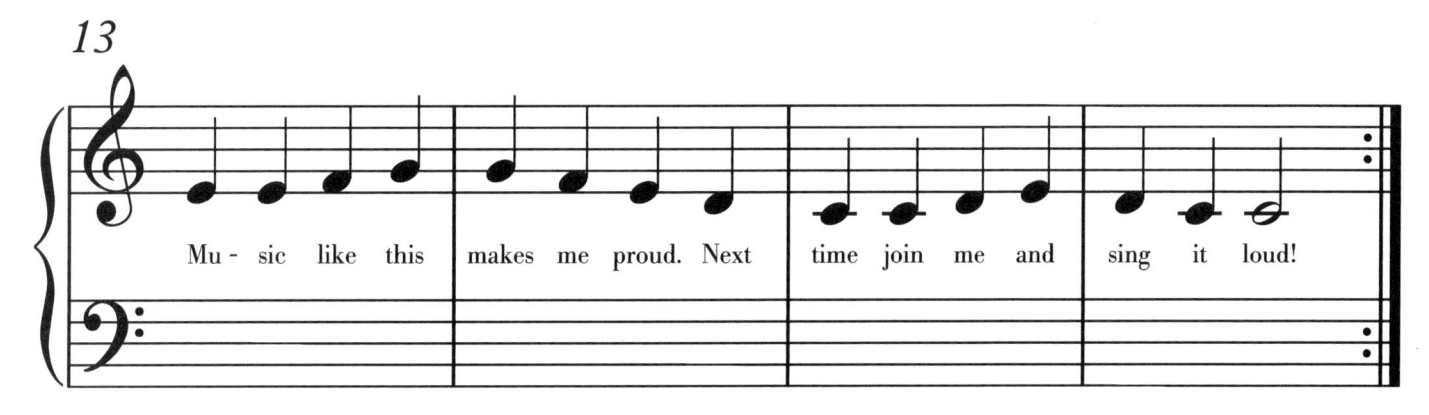

Ludwig van Beethoven
Lyrics by Jennifer Eklund

Quickly

Bee - tho - ven wrote lots of fa - mous mu - sic that I'll learn to play!

This one's called the "Ode to Joy." I'm hap - py to play this to - day!

This part's trick - y but it's my fav' - rite spot. Can't you tell I've worked a lot!

Mu - sic like this makes me proud. Next time join me and sing it loud!

Copyright © 2015 Piano Pronto Publishing, Inc.
All Rights Reserved | PianoPronto.com

Rests

Rests are used in music to notate silence. Look at the chart to learn three kinds of rests.

Quarter Rest = 1 beat of silence

Half Rest = 2 beats of silence

Whole Rest = 4 beats of silence (*or whole measure**)

*Later in this book you will learn about new time signatures that do not have 4 beats per measure. In these cases, a whole rest implies that the entire measure is silent.

Now It's Your Turn

♪ *Play the example below to practice playing with rests.*

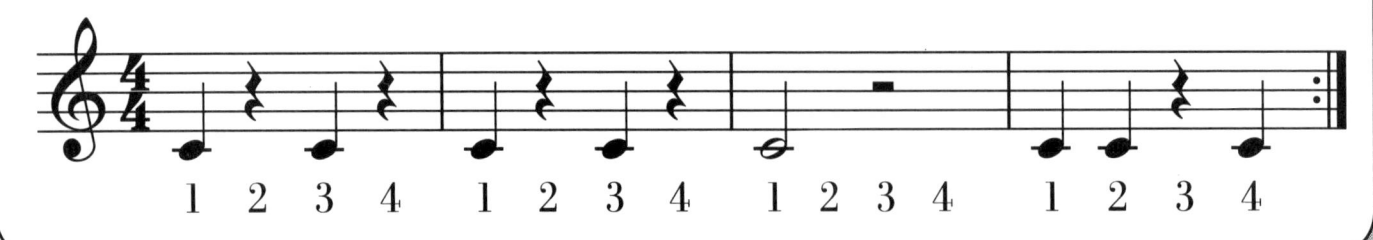

1 2 3 4   1 2 3 4   1 2 3 4   1 2 3 4

Before you begin:

♪ Circle the **quarter rests** in the next piece.

♪ Draw a box around the **half rests** in the next piece.

♪ Label the first note of each measure with the correct letter name.

11. On Your Toes!

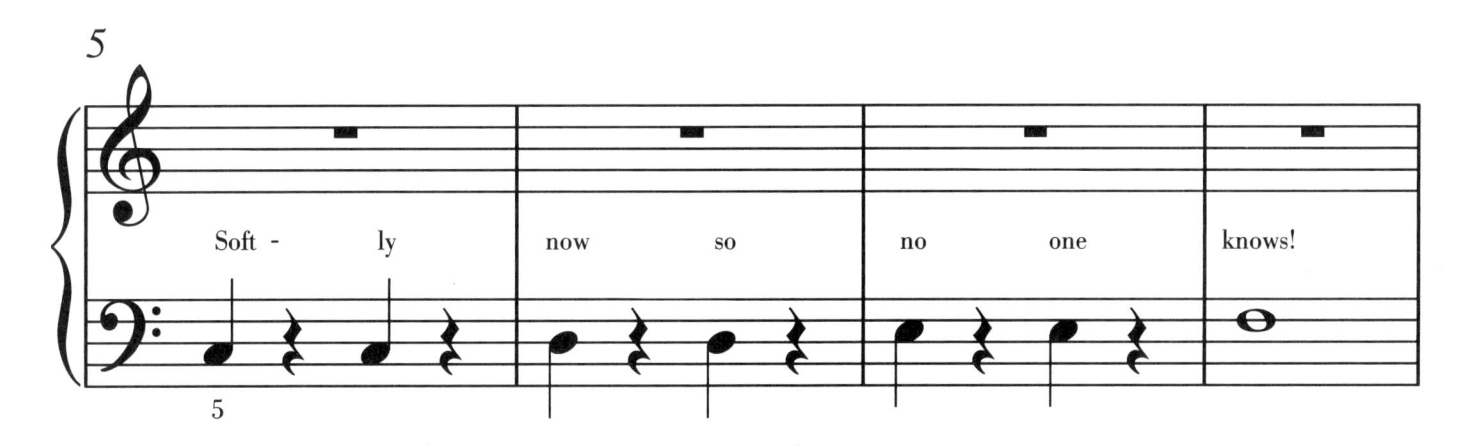

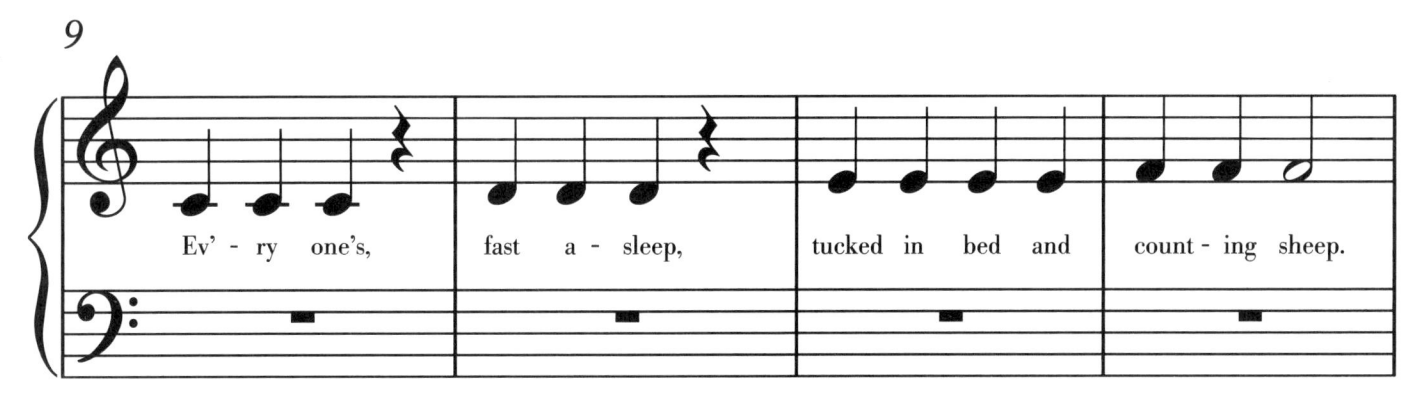

Music & Lyrics by
Jennifer Eklund

Quietly

On your toes, we creep so slow!

Soft-ly now so no one knows!

Ev'-ry one's, fast a-sleep, tucked in bed and count-ing sheep.

Got our snack, hur-ry back, on your toes!

Copyright © 2015 Piano Pronto Publishing, Inc.
All Rights Reserved | PianoPronto.com

New Note Combination

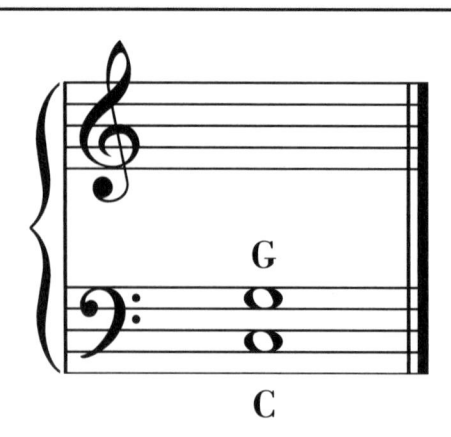

When notes are stacked on top of each other, play both keys at the same time.

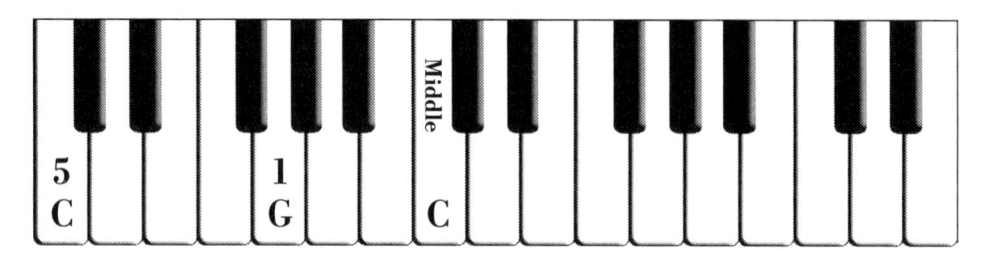

12. Pronto Prep

♪ *Play the examples below to help prepare for "Brother John."*

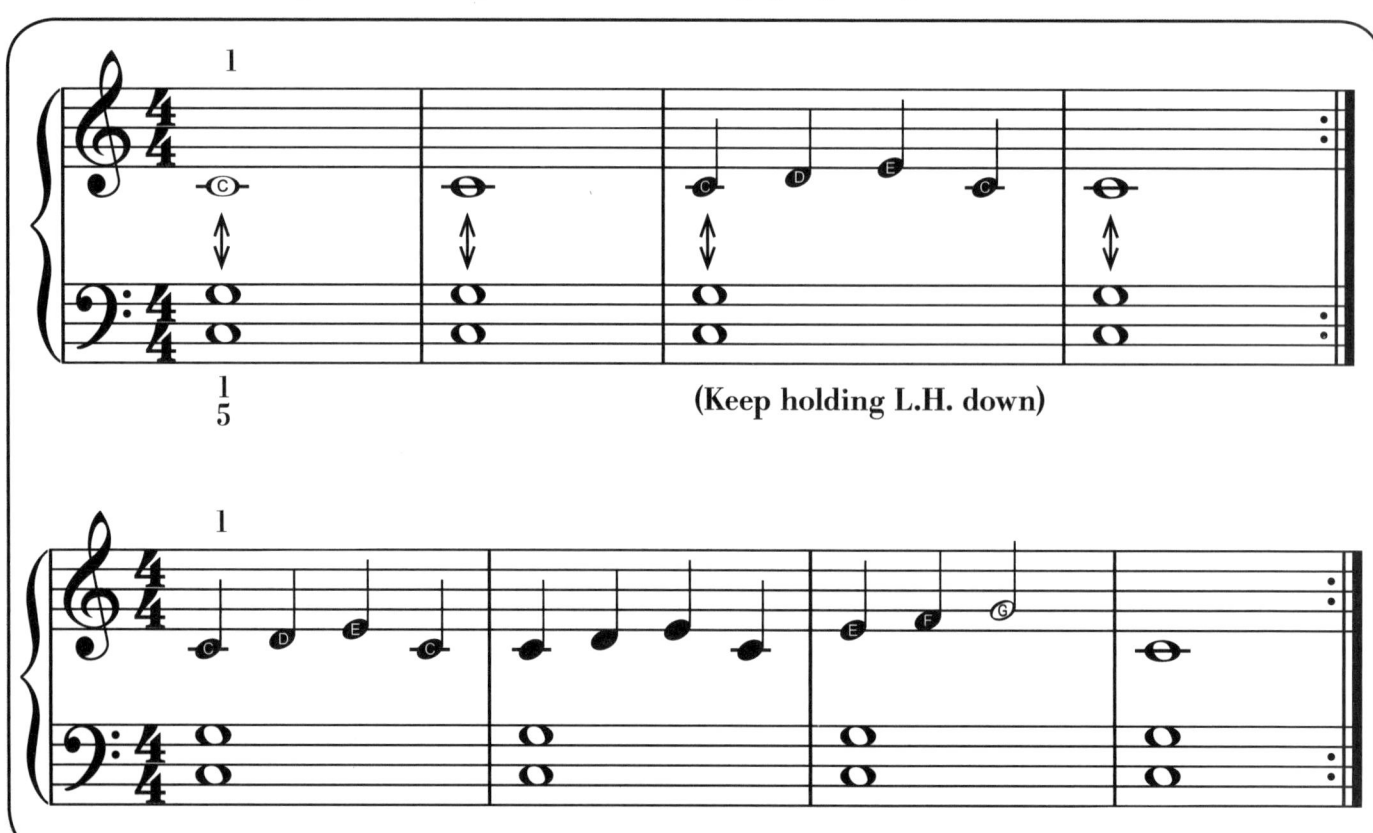

(Keep holding L.H. down)

12. Brother John

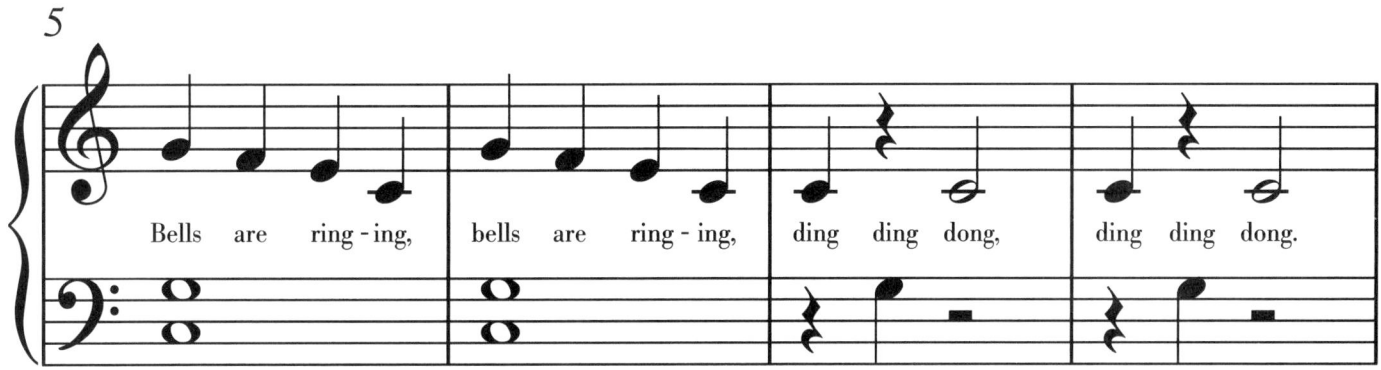

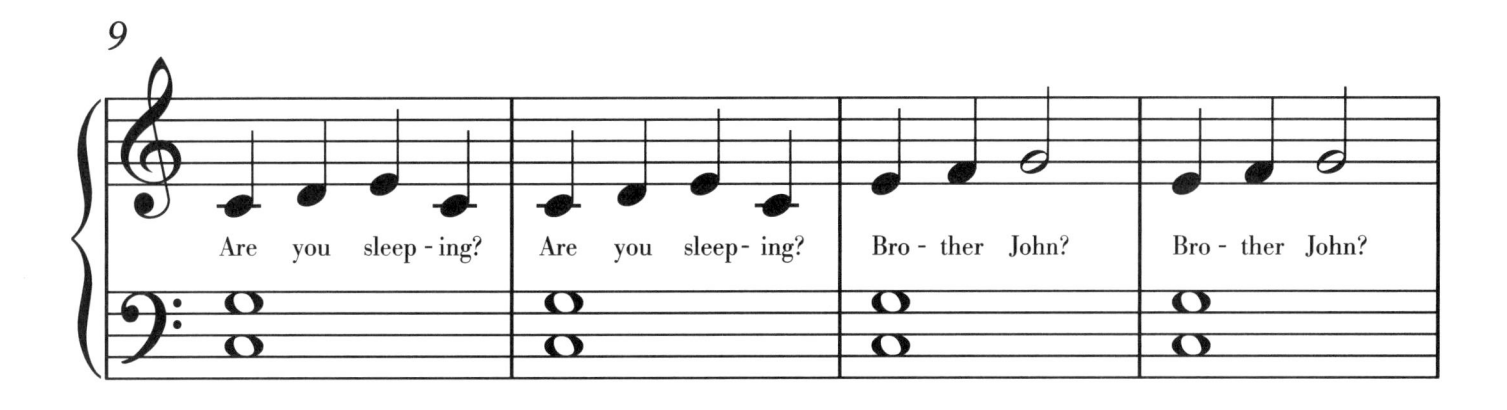

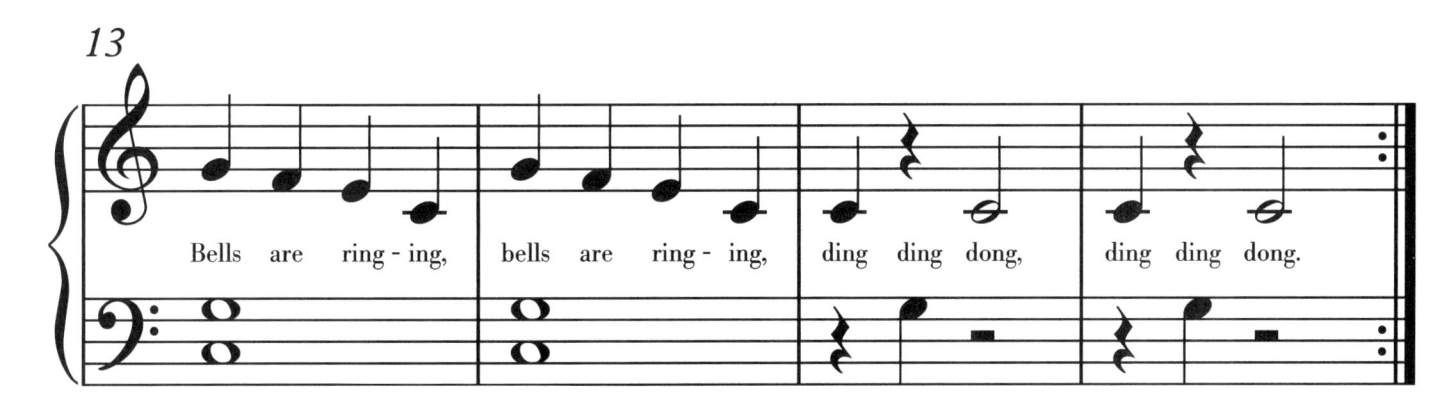

Traditional
Arr. Jennifer Eklund

Moderately

Are you sleep-ing? Are you sleep-ing? Bro-ther John? Bro-ther John?

Bells are ring-ing, bells are ring-ing, ding ding dong, ding ding dong.

Are you sleep-ing? Are you sleep-ing? Bro-ther John? Bro-ther John?

Bells are ring-ing, bells are ring-ing, ding ding dong, ding ding dong.

New Time Signature

3 beats per measure → **3**
4 ← Quarter note = 1 beat

Now It's Your Turn

♪ *Write in the missing barlines below. Watch the time signature!*

♪ *Write in the beat numbers below each measure.*

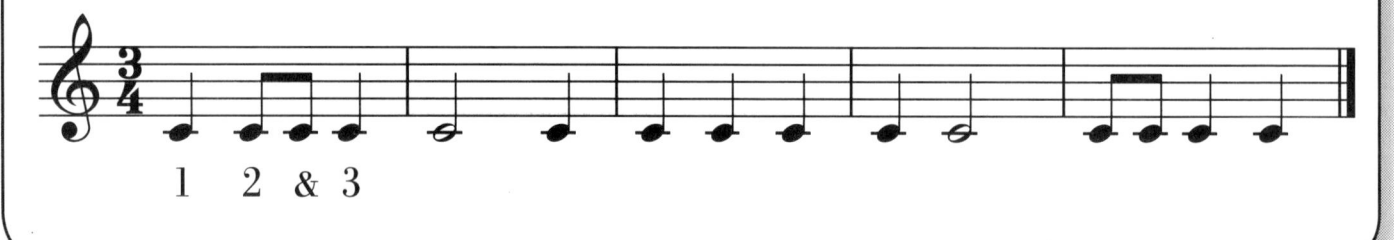

1　2　&　3

13. Pronto Prep

♪ *Play the example below to prepare for "Westminster Chimes."*

13. Westminster Chimes

Traditional
Arr. Jennifer Eklund

Moderately

Hear the clock chime, it tells the time. Count now with me, the time must be: one o' clock, two o' clock, three o' clock, four o' clock.

New Note Combination

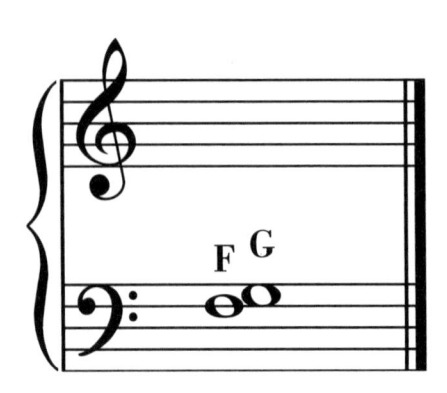

When notes are stacked on top of each other, play both keys at the same time.

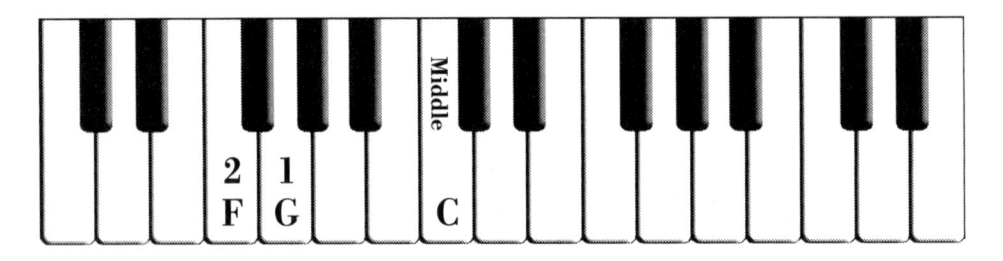

14. Pronto Prep

♫ *Play the examples below to help prepare for "Hot Cross Buns."*

14. Hot Cross Buns

Traditional
Arr. Jennifer Eklund

Quickly

Copyright © 2015 Piano Pronto Publishing, Inc.
All Rights Reserved | PianoPronto.com

Treble Clef Word Puzzle

♪ *Write the correct letter name below each note. Every measure will spell a word.*

E G G

15. Pronto Prep

♪ *Play the examples below to help prepare for "Rain, Rain, Go Away."*

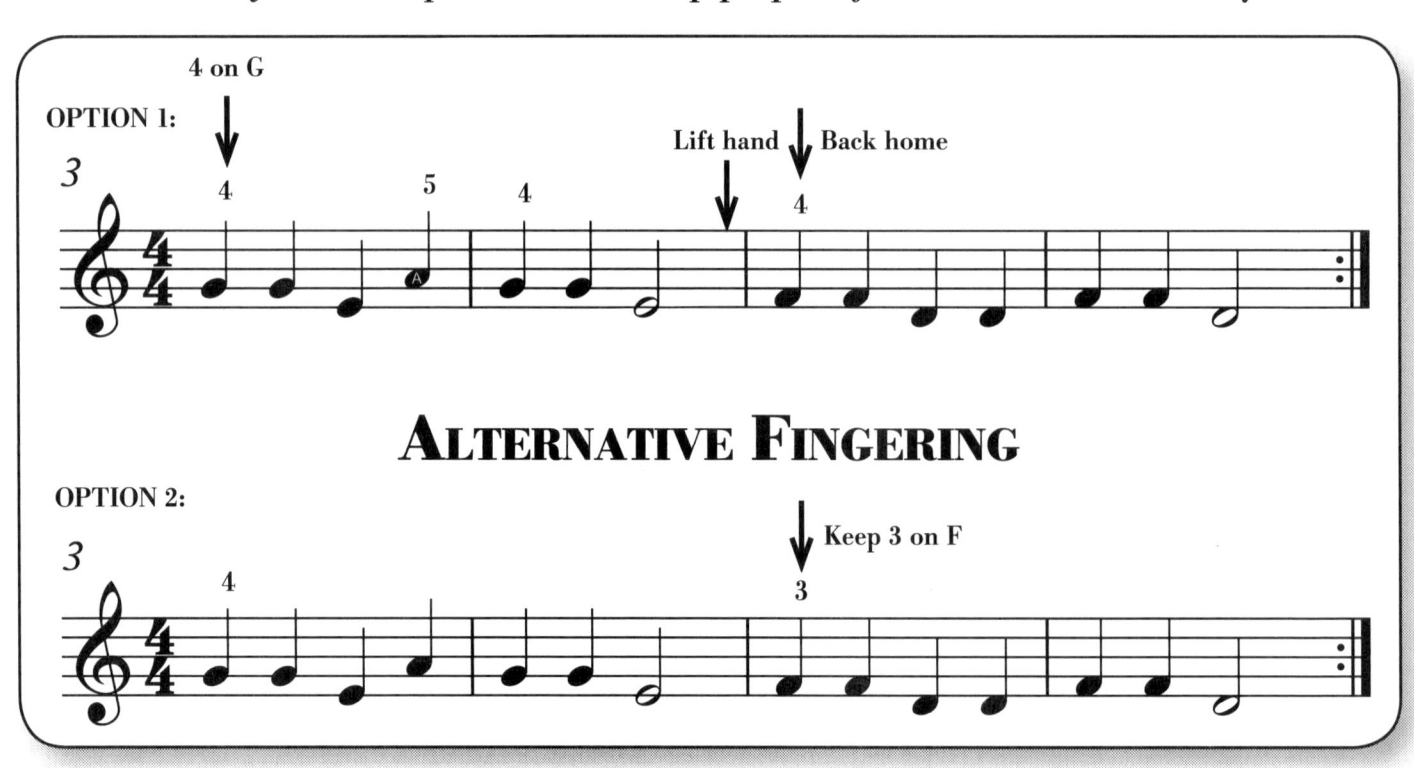

OPTION 1:

4 on G — 4, 5, 4, Lift hand, Back home — 4

ALTERNATIVE FINGERING

OPTION 2:

4, Keep 3 on F — 3

Before you begin:

♪ Write in the fingerings you chose for **measure 5** before you play.

15. Rain, Rain, Go Away

Traditional
Arr. Jennifer Eklund

Sadly

Copyright © 2015 Piano Pronto Publishing, Inc.
All Rights Reserved | PianoPronto.com

Dynamics

Dynamic markings describe how loudly or softly to play the music. Look at the chart below to learn two dynamic markings, their Italian names, and English translation.

p = *piano* = play softly

f = *forte* = play loudly

Now It's Your Turn

♪ *Play the example below following the dynamic markings.*

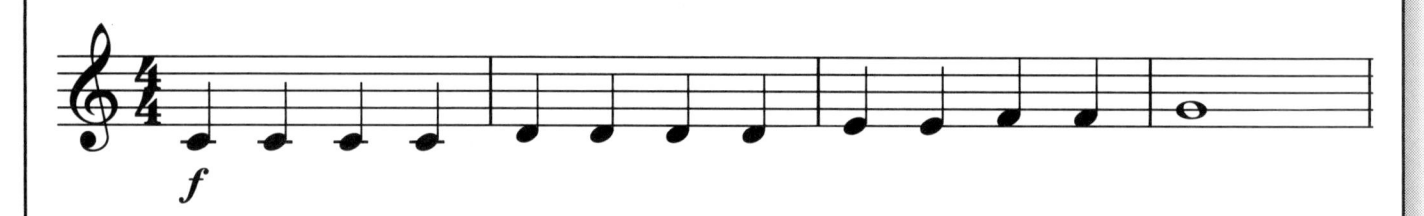

f

p

Before you begin:

♪ What is the **dynamic marking** in the next piece? _____

♪ This **dynamic marking** means to play _____.

♪ What is the **tempo (speed)** of the next piece? _____

16. River Road

Antonín Dvořák
Arr. Jennifer Eklund

Very slowly

p Ri - ver road, ri - ver road,

wind - ing to the sea.

Ri - ver road, ri - ver road,

where I long to be.

New Note Combination

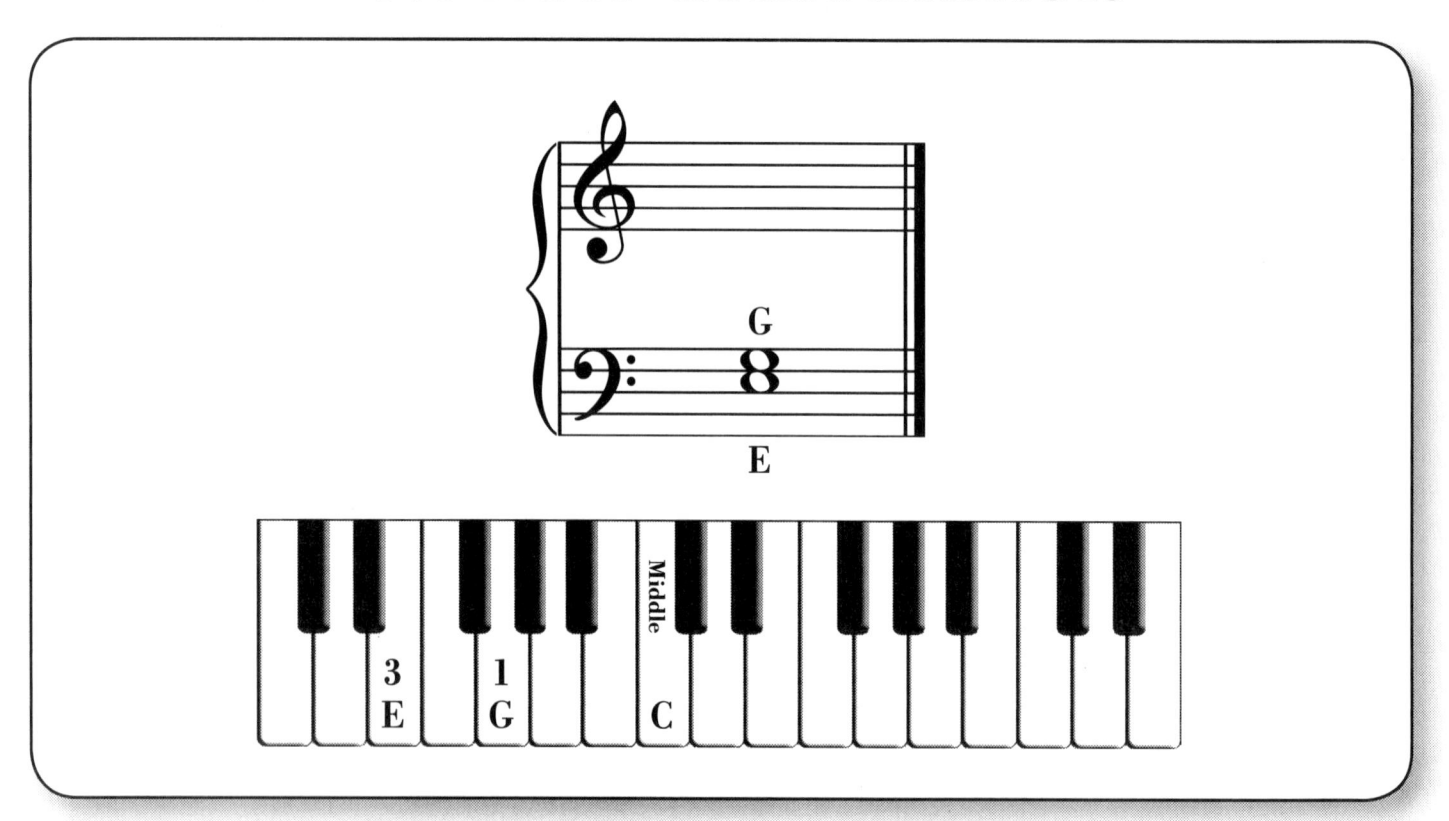

17. Pronto Prep

♪ *Play the examples below to help prepare for "Merrily We Roll Along."*

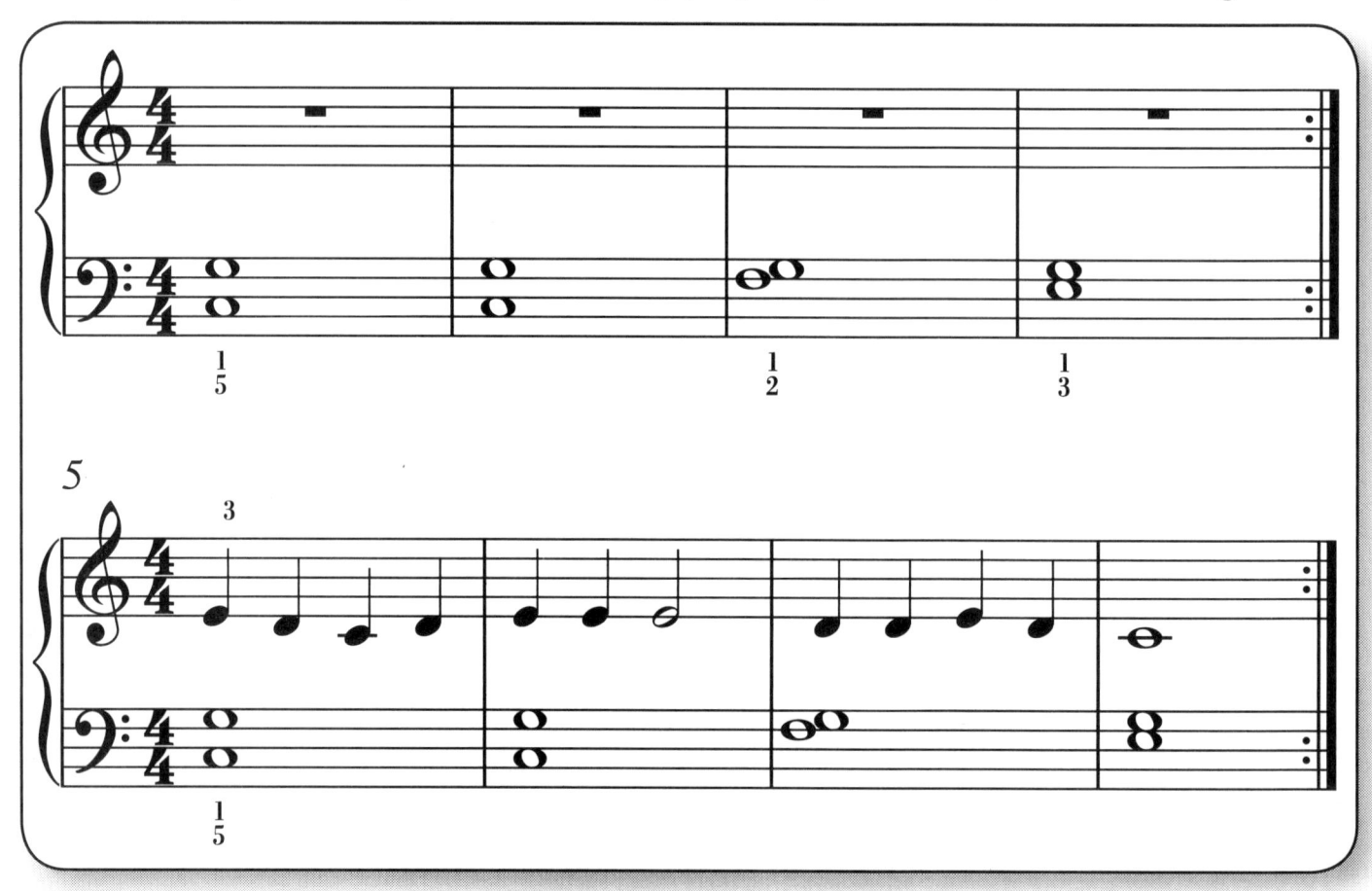

17. Merrily We Roll Along

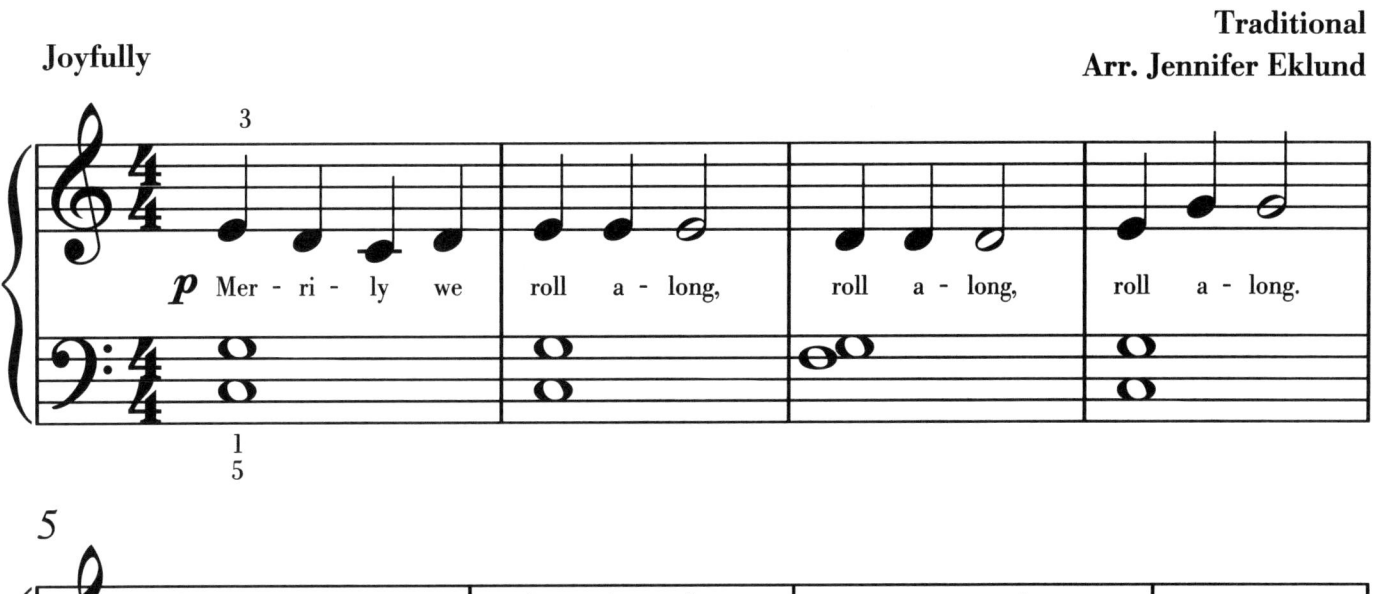

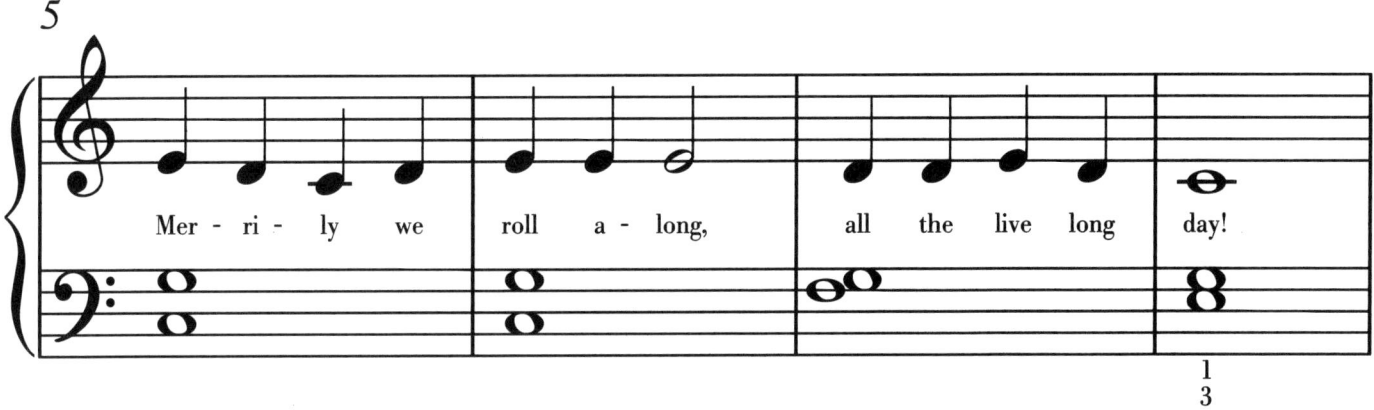

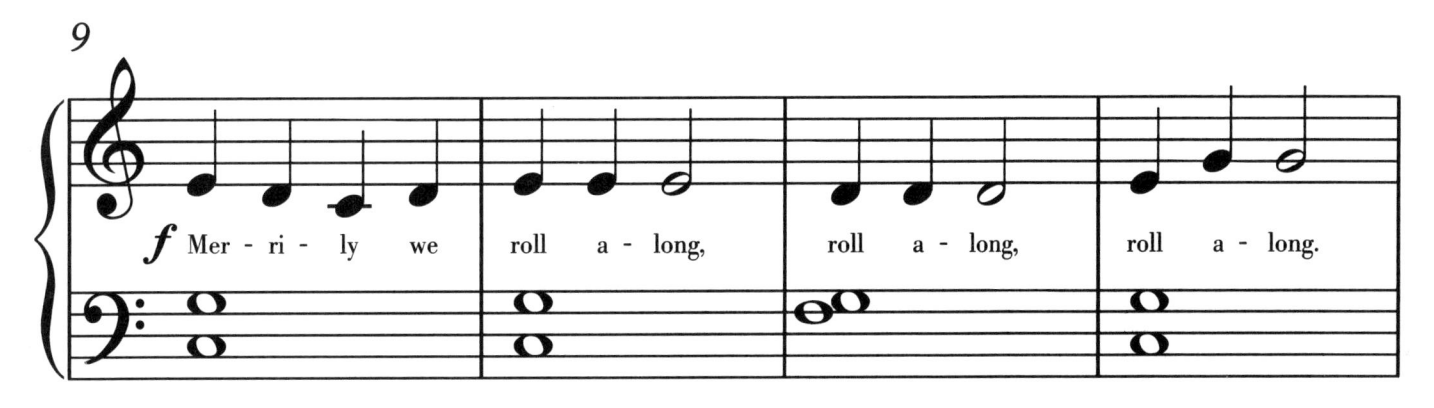

Traditional
Arr. Jennifer Eklund

Joyfully

Mer-ri-ly we roll a-long, roll a-long, roll a-long.

Mer-ri-ly we roll a-long, all the live long day!

Mer-ri-ly we roll a-long, roll a-long, roll a-long.

Mer-ri-ly we roll a-long, all the live long day!

Ties

A **tie** is a line that connects two notes of the same pitch (*same position on the staff*). When notes are tied, you strike the first note, but do NOT strike the second note. Study the examples below.

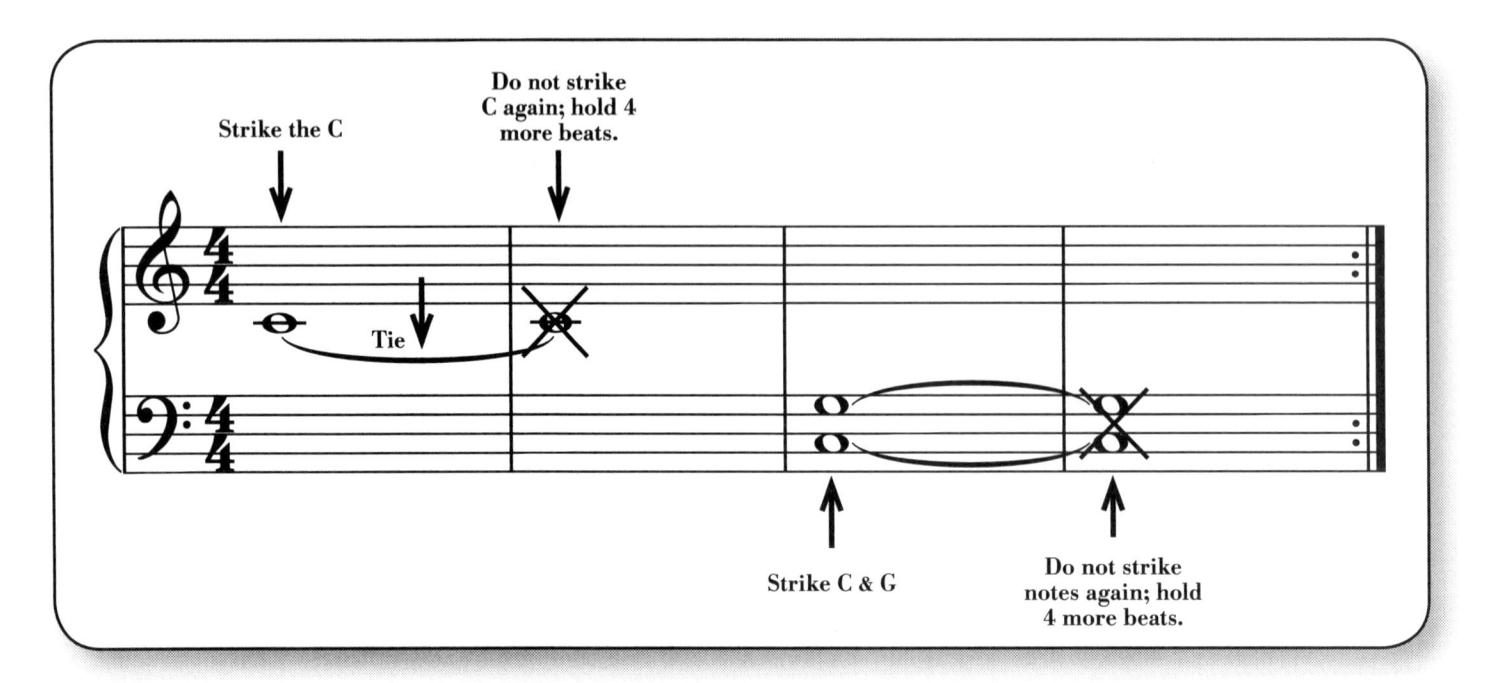

18. Pronto Prep

♪ *Play the examples below to help prepare for "Lightly Row."*

18. Lightly Row

Traditional
Arr. Jennifer Eklund

Moderately

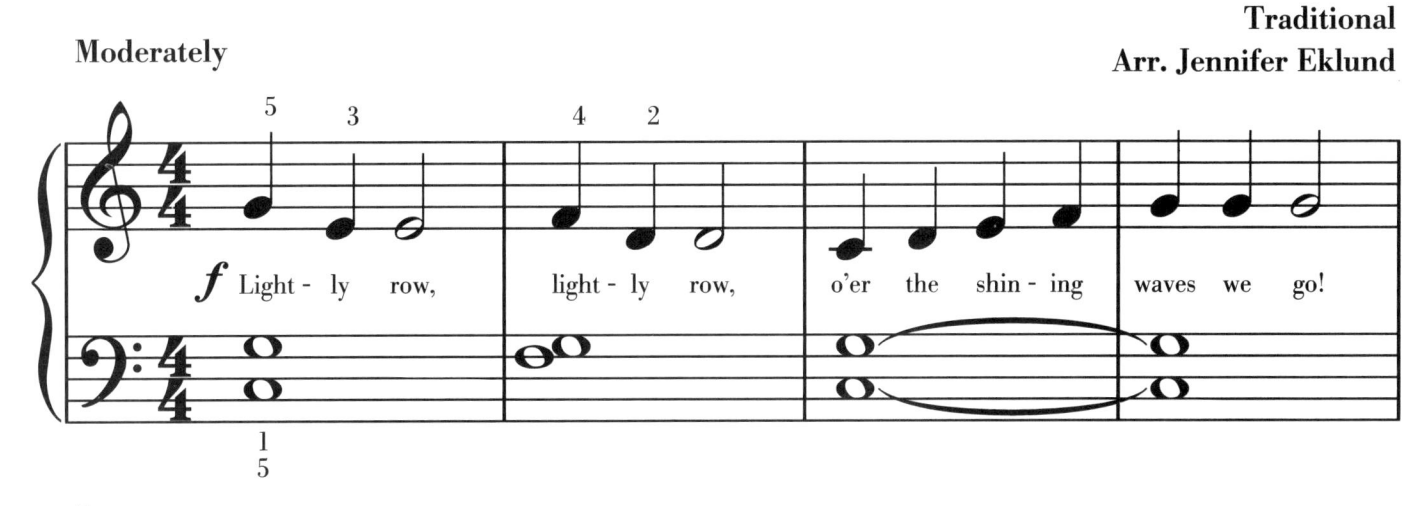

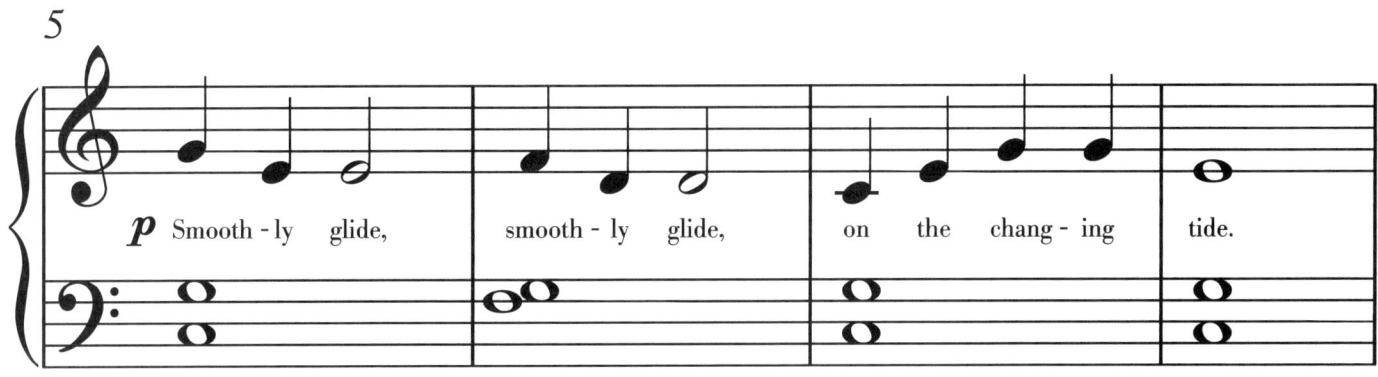

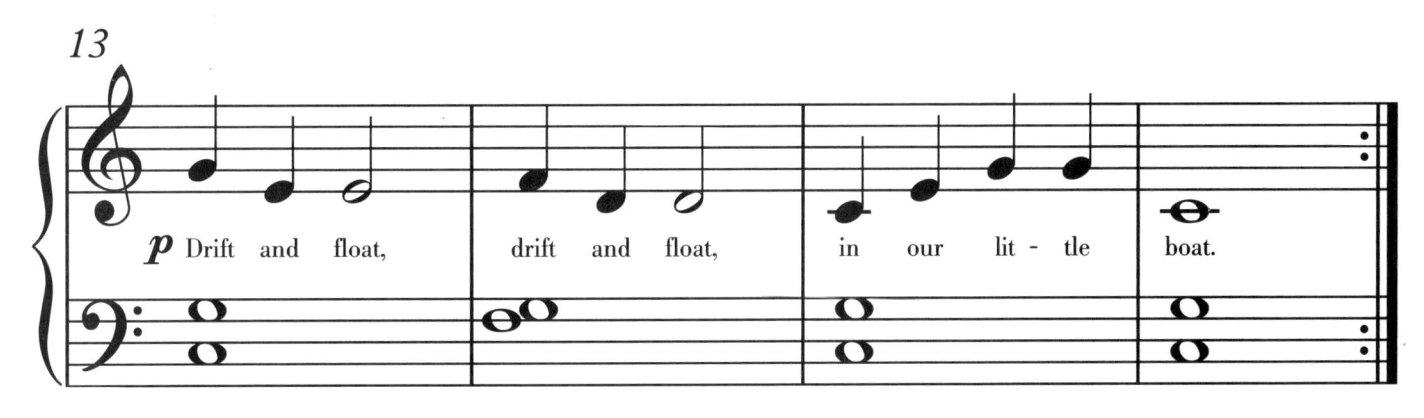

f Light-ly row, light-ly row, o'er the shin-ing waves we go!

p Smooth-ly glide, smooth-ly glide, on the chang-ing tide.

f Let the winds and wa-ter be, still and calm and clear to see.

p Drift and float, drift and float, in our lit-tle boat.

New Rhythms

Dotted quarter note = 1½ beats

NOTE: A dot adds half the value of the note it is attached to.

Dotted quarter notes are often put together with eighth notes to make a total of 2 beats.

♩. + ♪ = 2 beats

Now It's Your Turn

♪ *Play the example below. You can count out this rhythm with numbers or words.*

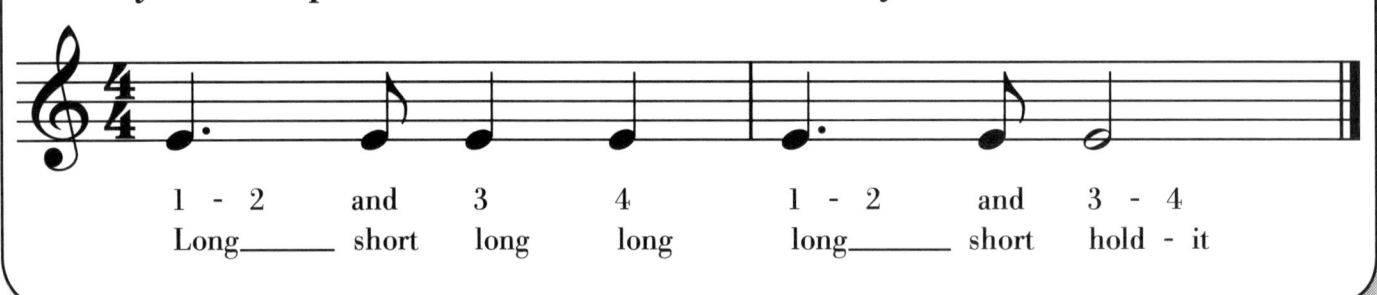

1 - 2	and	3	4	1 - 2	and	3 - 4
Long	short	long	long	long	short	hold - it

19. Pronto Prep

♪ *Play the example below to help prepare for "London Bridge."*

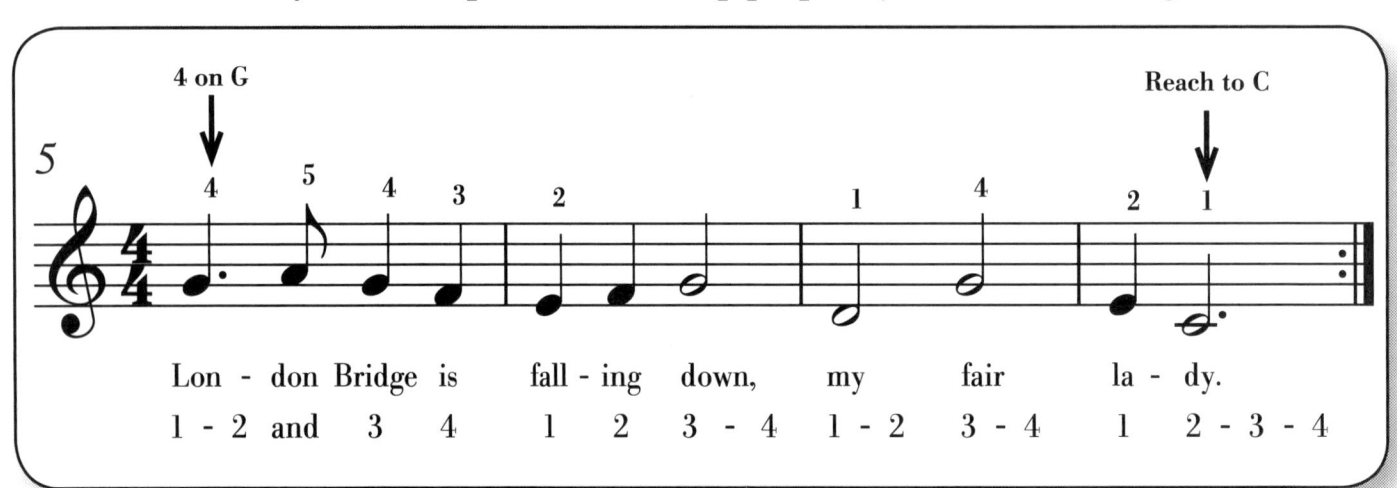

4 on G — Reach to C

Lon - don Bridge is fall - ing down, my fair la - dy.
1 - 2 and 3 4 1 2 3 - 4 1 - 2 3 - 4 1 2 - 3 - 4

19. London Bridge

Traditional
Arr. Jennifer Eklund

Joyfully

New Note

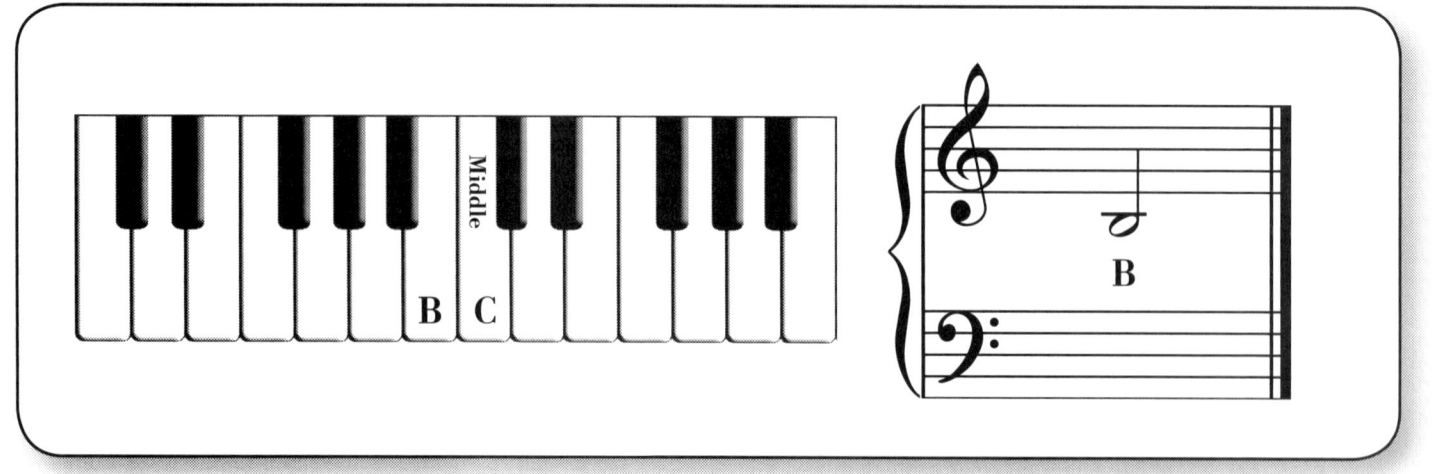

Now It's Your Turn

Two fingerings can be used to play the B. Both of these occur in the next song.

20. Pronto Prep

♪ *Play the examples below to help prepare for "On the Bridge at Avignon."*

20. On the Bridge at Avignon

Traditional
Arr. Jennifer Eklund

Moderately

Rhythm Review

MATCHING

♪   Quarter note

♩   Whole rest

▬   Eighth note

𝅗𝅥   Half note

▬   Dotted quarter note

𝅗𝅥.   Whole note

𝅝   Quarter rest

𝄽   Dotted half note

♩.   2 eighth notes

♫   Half rest

21. Hush, Little Baby

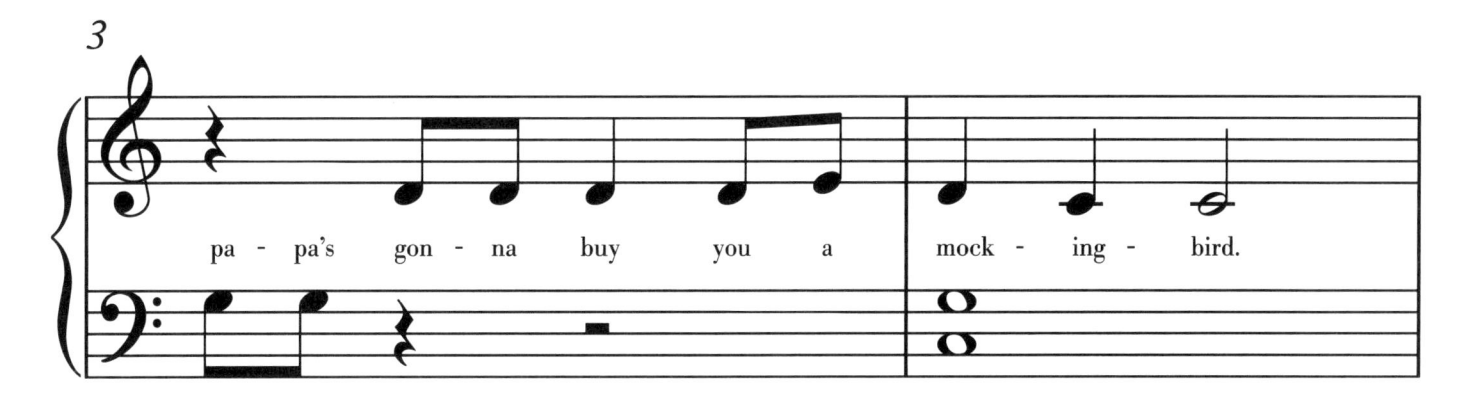

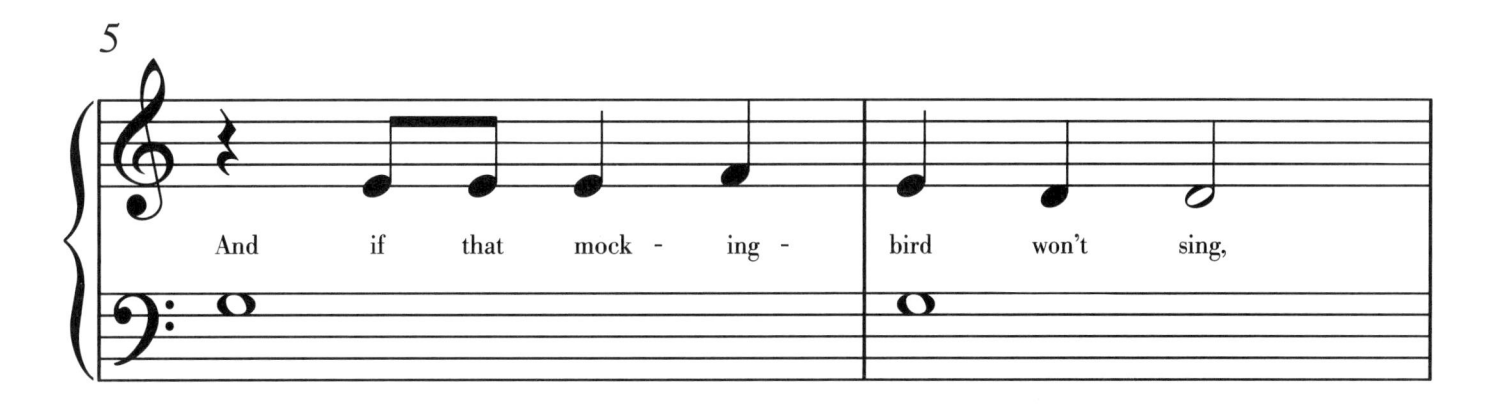

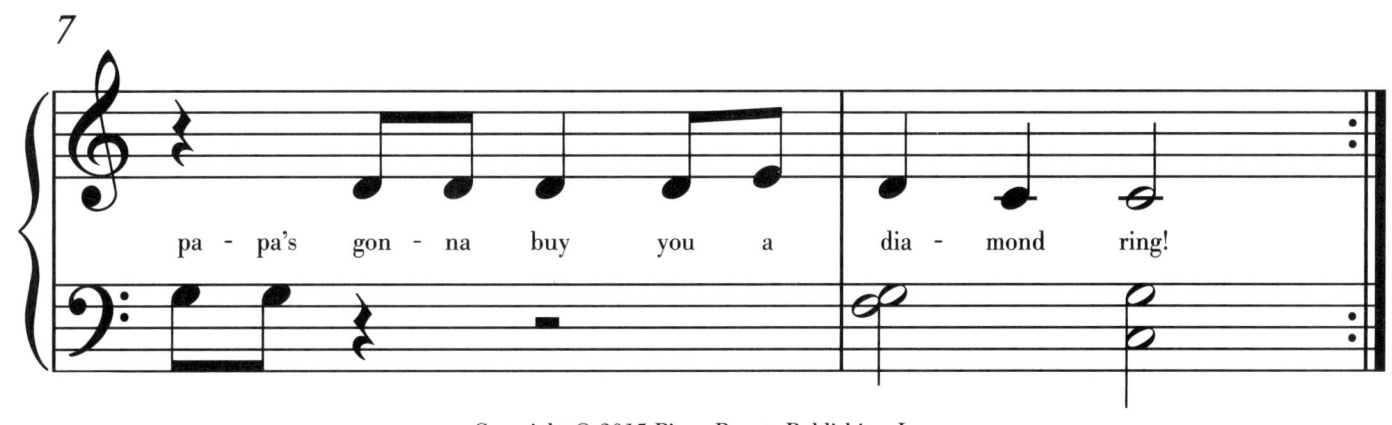

Traditional
Arr. Jennifer Eklund

Slowly

New Dynamics

mp = *mezzo piano* = medium soft

mf = *mezzo forte* = medium loud

MATCHING

f	*piano*	loud
p	*mezzo forte*	medium soft
mf	*forte*	soft
mp	*mezzo piano*	medium loud

22. Pronto Prep

♪ *Play the example below to help prepare for "Down in the Valley."*

22. Down in the Valley

Traditional
Arr. Jennifer Eklund

Moderately fast

mf Down in the val - ley, val - ley so low,

hang your head o - ver, hear the wind blow.

mp Ros - es love sun - shine, vio - lets love dew.

An - gels in heav - en know I love you!

49

New Notes

The next piece uses a new combination of bass clef notes, and a new treble clef note.

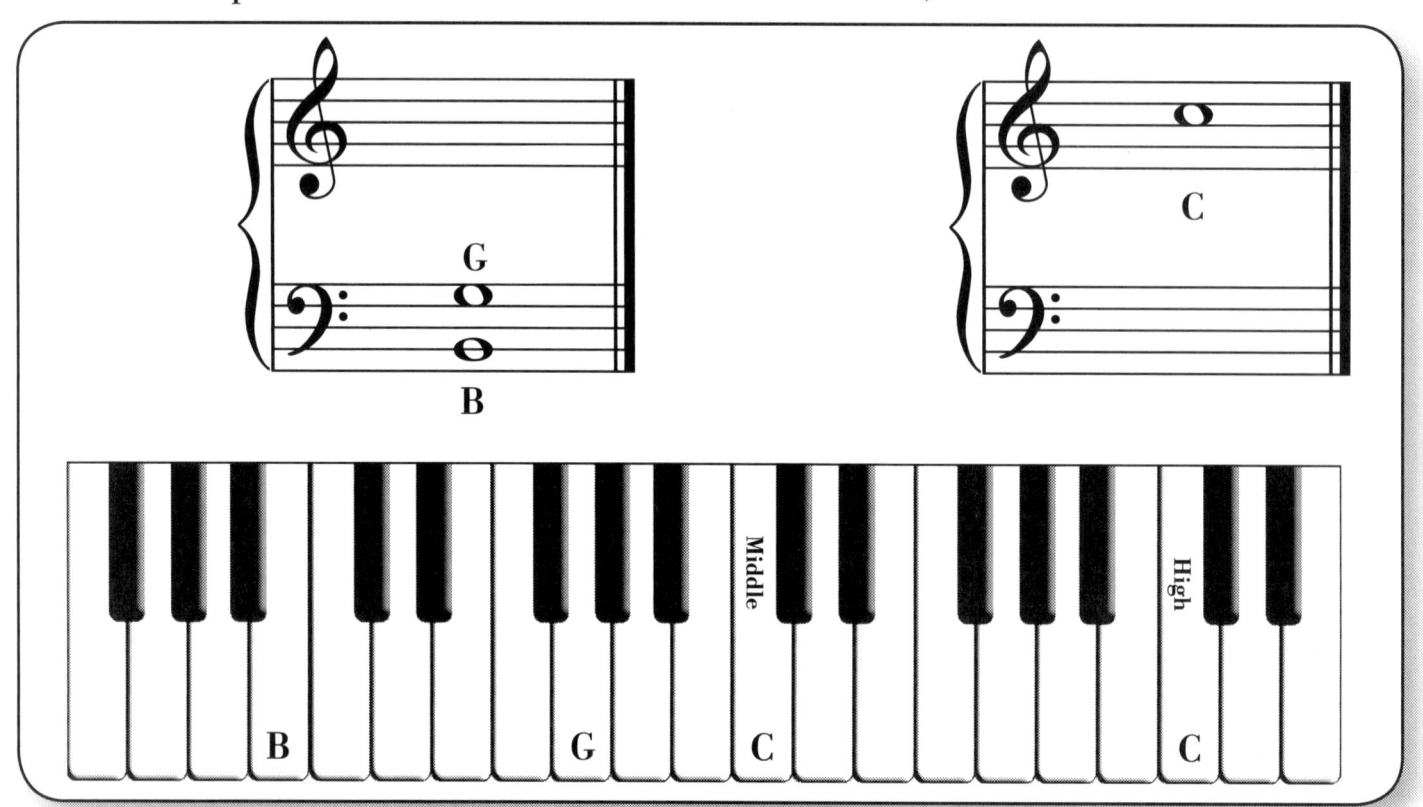

23. Pronto Prep

♪ *Play the examples below to help prepare for "Row, Row, Row Your Boat."*

23. Row, Row, Row Your Boat

Traditional
Arr. Jennifer Eklund

Quickly

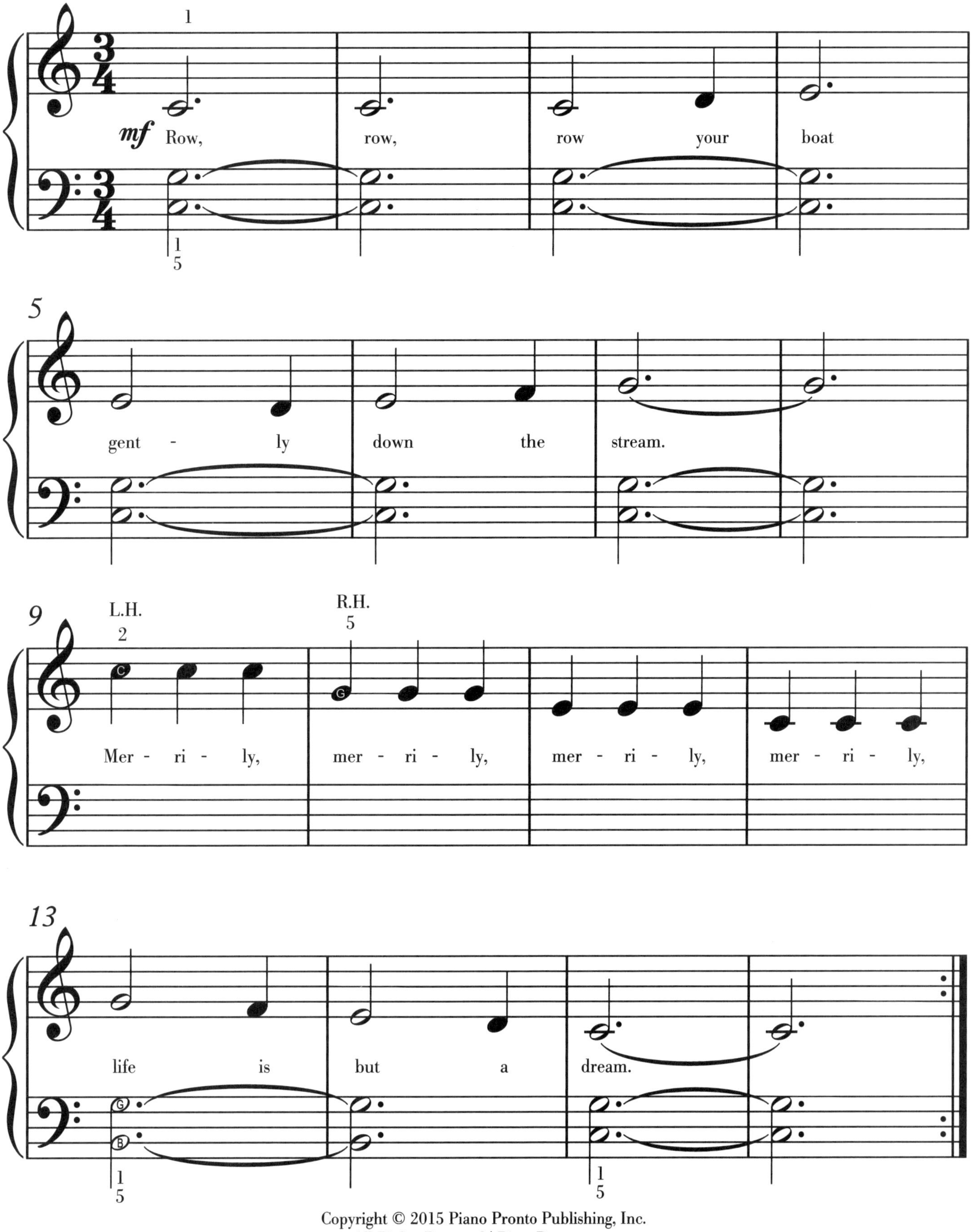

Copyright © 2015 Piano Pronto Publishing, Inc.
All Rights Reserved | PianoPronto.com

New Time Signature

2 beats per measure → **2**
4 ← Quarter note = 1 beat

Now It's Your Turn

♪ *Write in the missing barlines below. Watch the time signature!*

♪ *Write in the beat numbers below each measure.*

1 2 &

24. Pronto Prep

♪ *Play the example below to help prepare for "Skip to My Lou."*

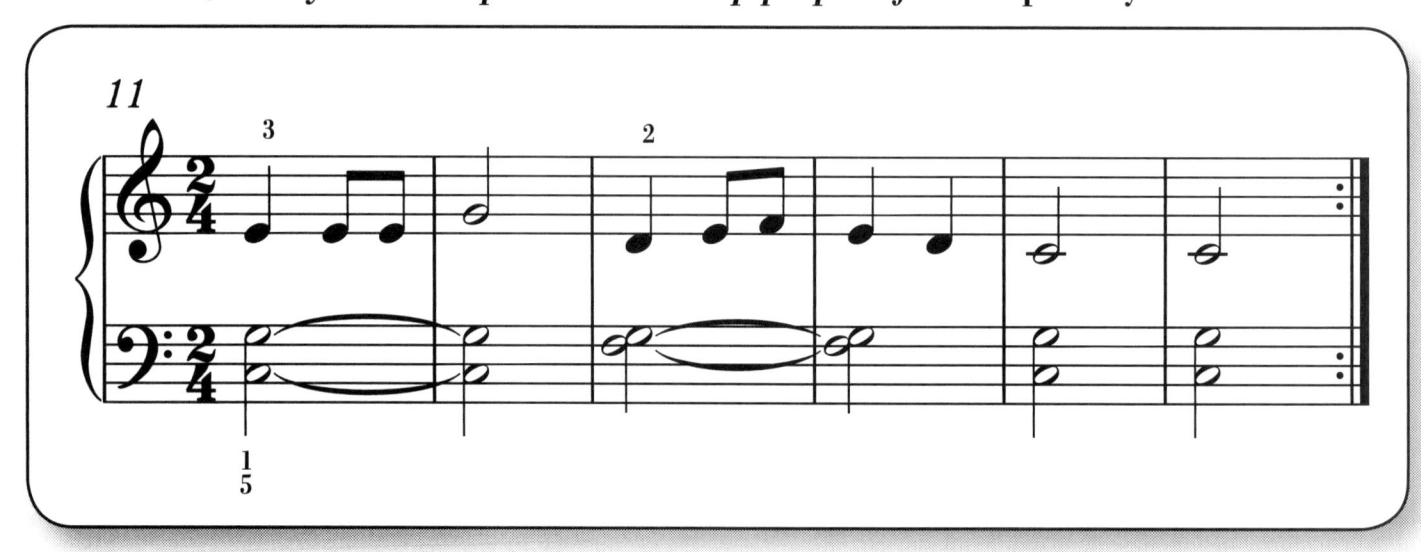

24. Skip to My Lou

Traditional
Arr. Jennifer Eklund

Moderately

Lou, Lou, skip to my Lou.
Lou, Lou, skip to my Lou.
Lou, Lou, skip to my Lou.
Skip to my Lou, my dar - lin'.

New Note Combination

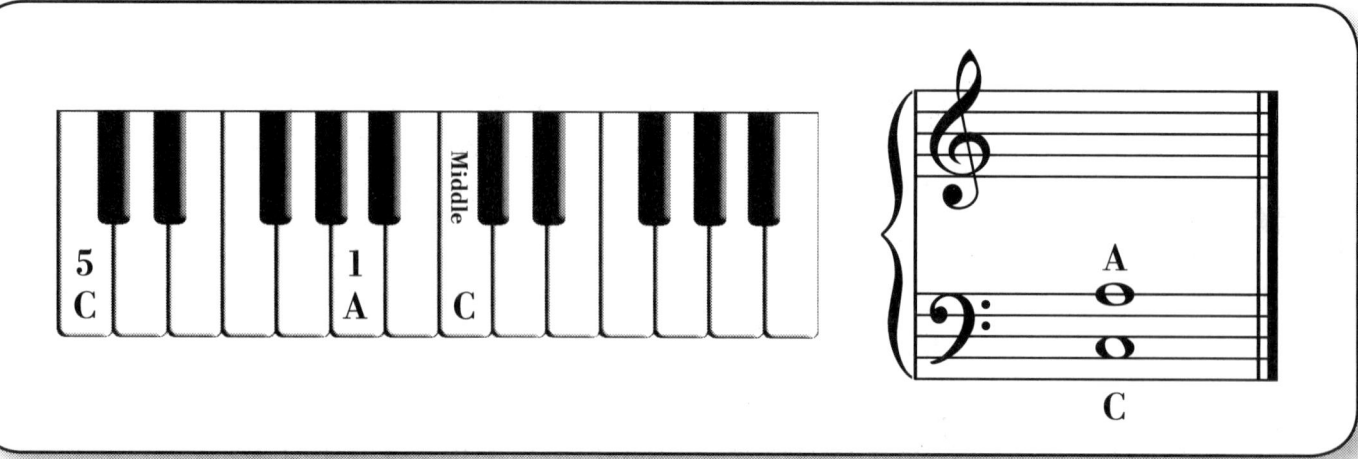

25. Pronto Prep

♪ *Play the examples below to help prepare for "Oh, Susannah."*

OPTION 1:

ALTERNATIVE FINGERING

OPTION 2:

Before you begin:

♪ Write in the fingerings you chose in the music before you play.

INCOMPLETE MEASURES

The next piece begins with a measure that does not have enough beats. These notes lead into the main melody and are called **pick-up notes**. The missing beats are usually found in the last measure of the piece.

25. Oh, Susannah

Stephen Foster
Arr. Jennifer Eklund

Quickly

mf Well, I come from Al - a - ba - ma with a ban - jo on my knee. And I'm bound for Loui - si - an - a, my own true love for to see.

f Oh, Su - san - nah, oh don't you cry for me, as I come from Al - a - ba - ma with a ban - jo on my knee.

New Note Combination

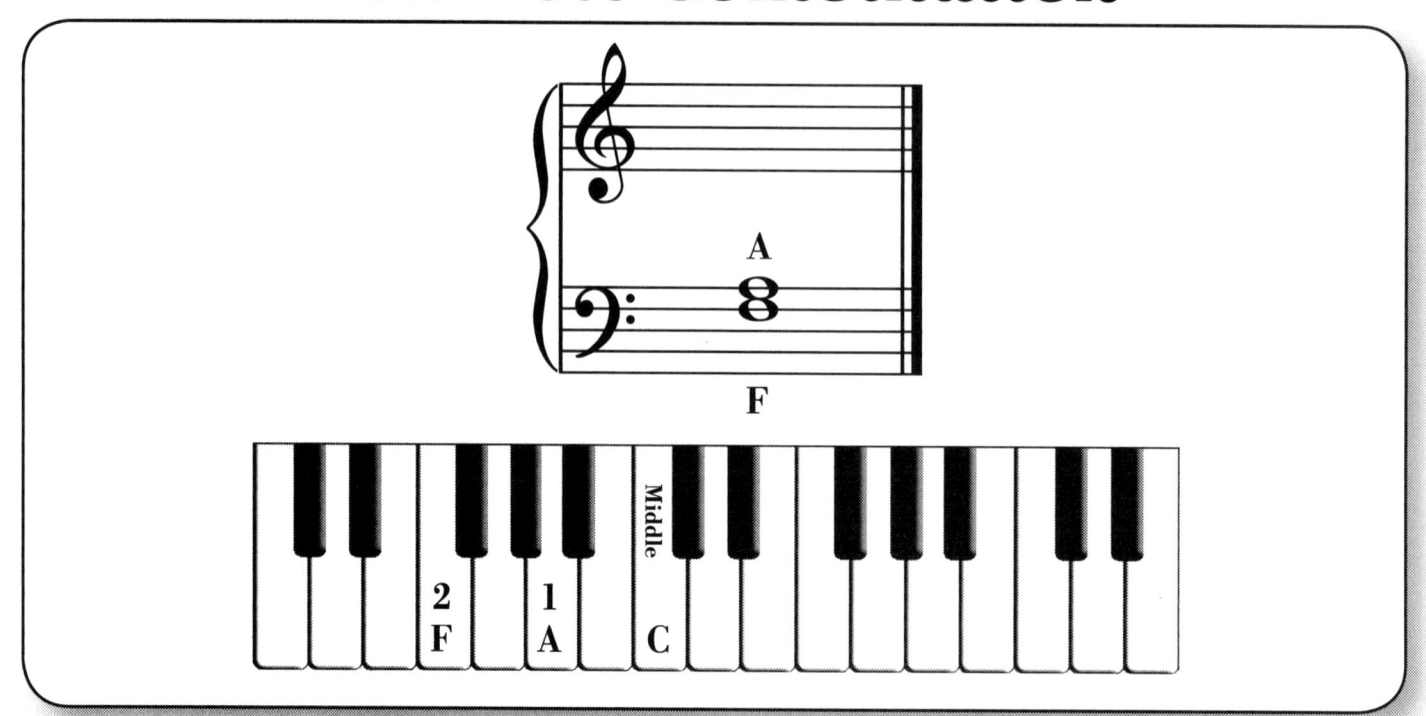

26. Pronto Prep

♪ *Play the examples below to help prepare for "Old MacDonald."*

26. Old MacDonald

Traditional
Arr. Jennifer Eklund

Joyfully

Bass Clef Word Puzzle

♪ *Write the correct letter name below each note. Every measure will spell a word.*

E G G

Draw the Barlines

♪ *Write in the missing barlines. Watch the time signatures and the ties!*

Slurs

A **slur** is a curved line that connects two or more notes, and indicates that these notes should be played **legato**. Legato means to play smoothly without a break in between the notes. Try the example below.

Tie or Slur?

Remember that unlike **slurs**, a **tie** connects two notes that share the same pitch (same position on the staff). Label each measure below as a tie or slur.

27. Pronto Prep

♪ *Play the example below to help prepare for "Morning Theme."*

27. Morning Theme

Edvard Grieg
Arr. Jennifer Eklund

Moderately slow

60

Half Steps & Whole Steps

Half step = the very next key up or down

Whole step = two half steps

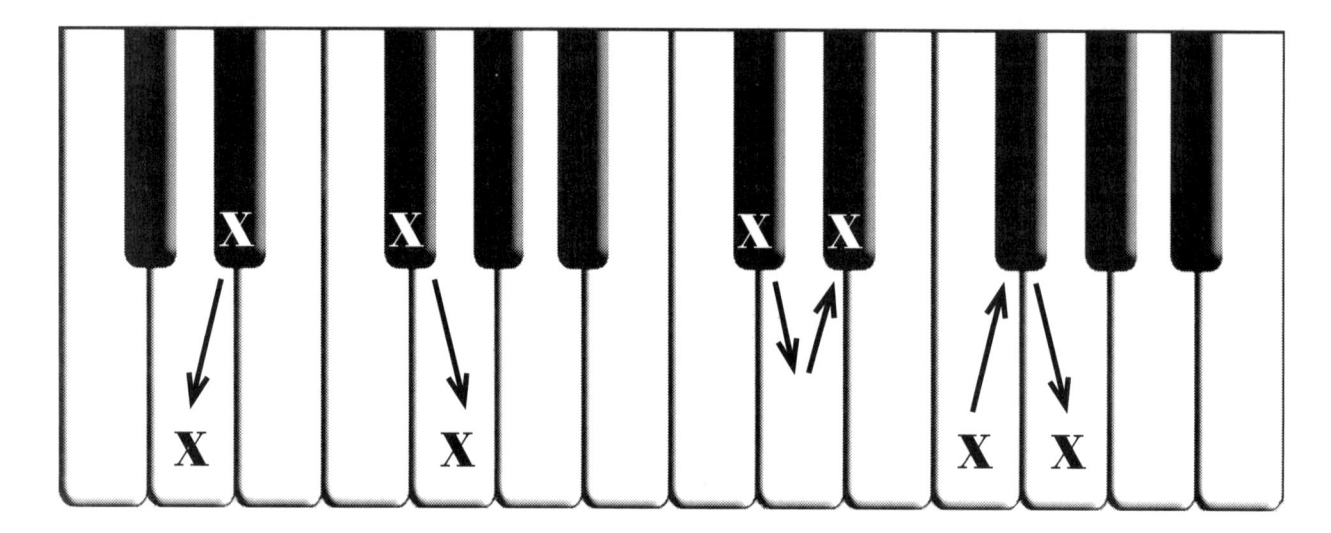

Half steps   Whole steps

Now It's Your Turn

♪ *Label each pair of X's as a **half step** or **whole step**.*

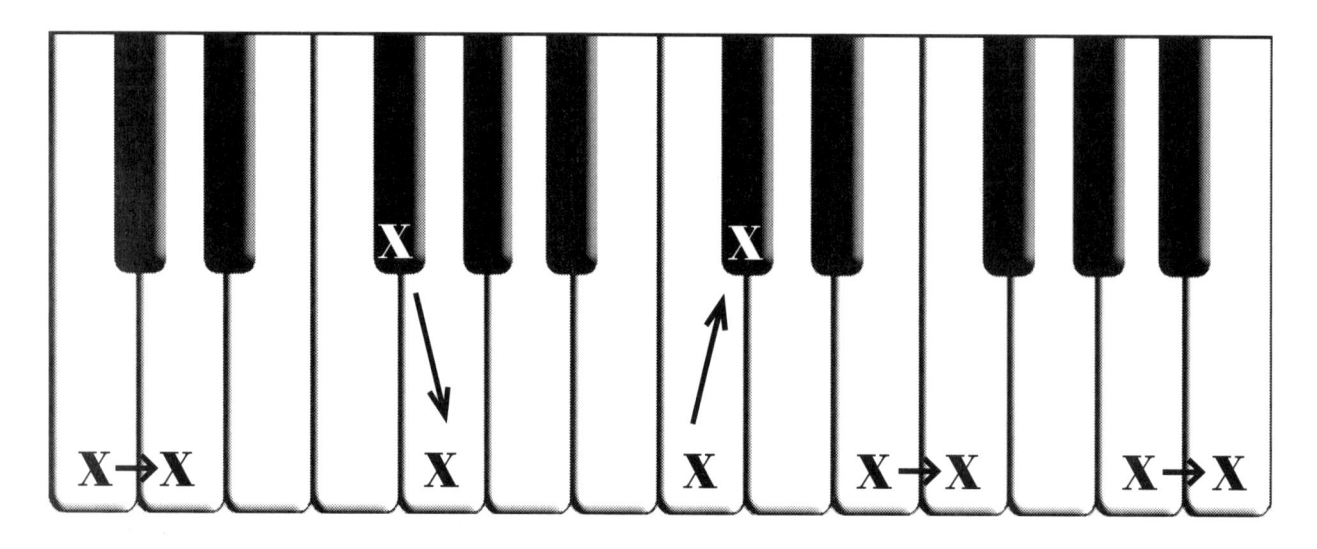

_____   _____   _____

Flats

♭ = Flat sign = play the key a half step lower

New Note

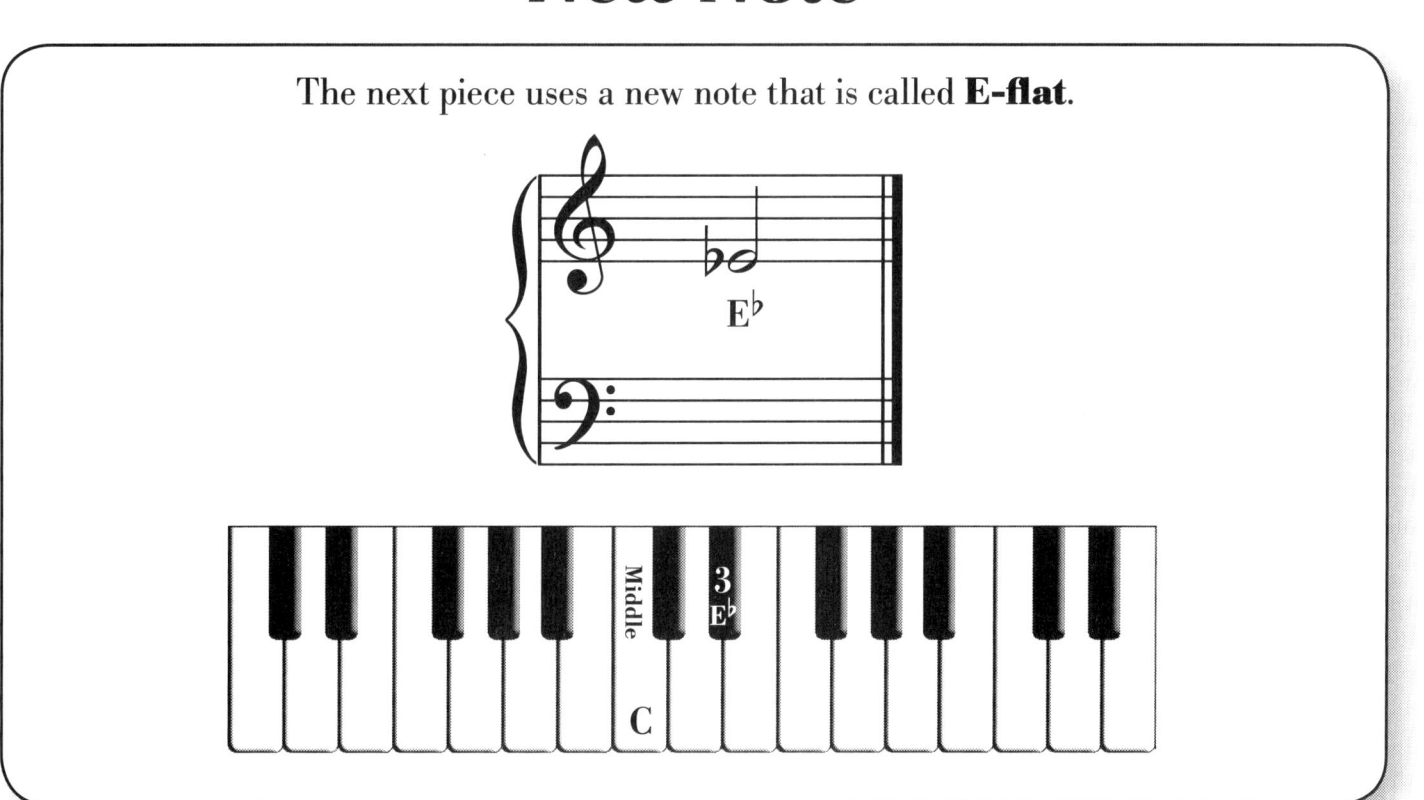

The next piece uses a new note that is called **E-flat**.

28. Pronto Prep

♪ *Play the example below to help prepare for "Snake Dance."*

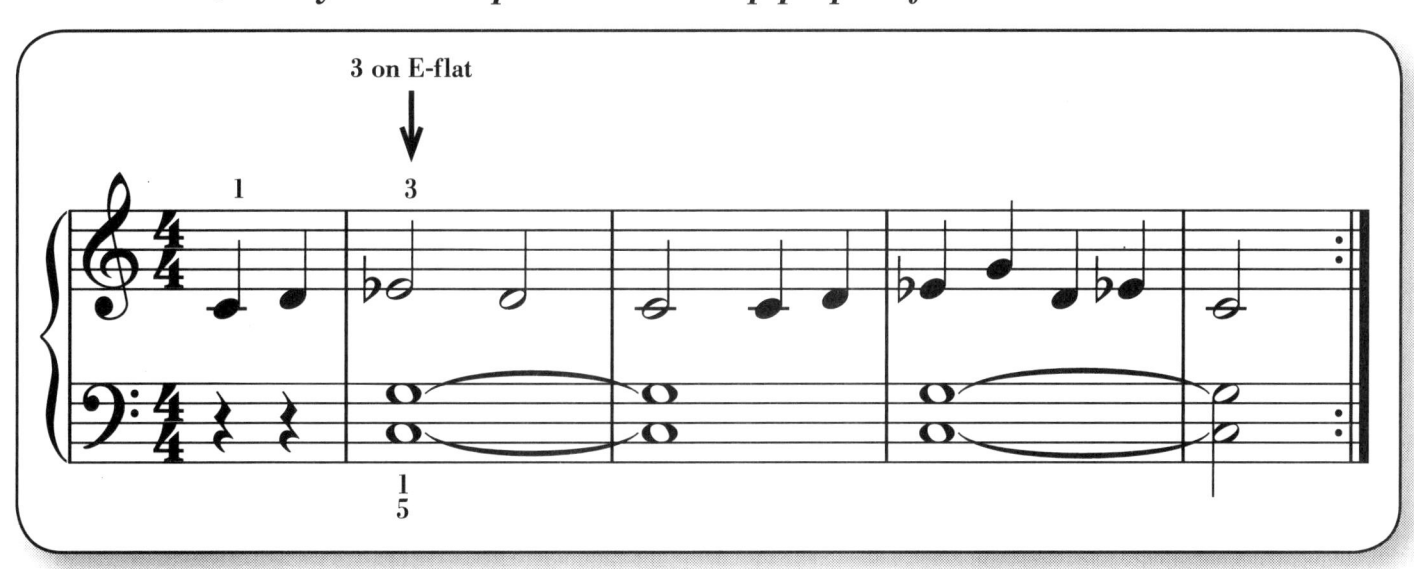

28. Snake Dance

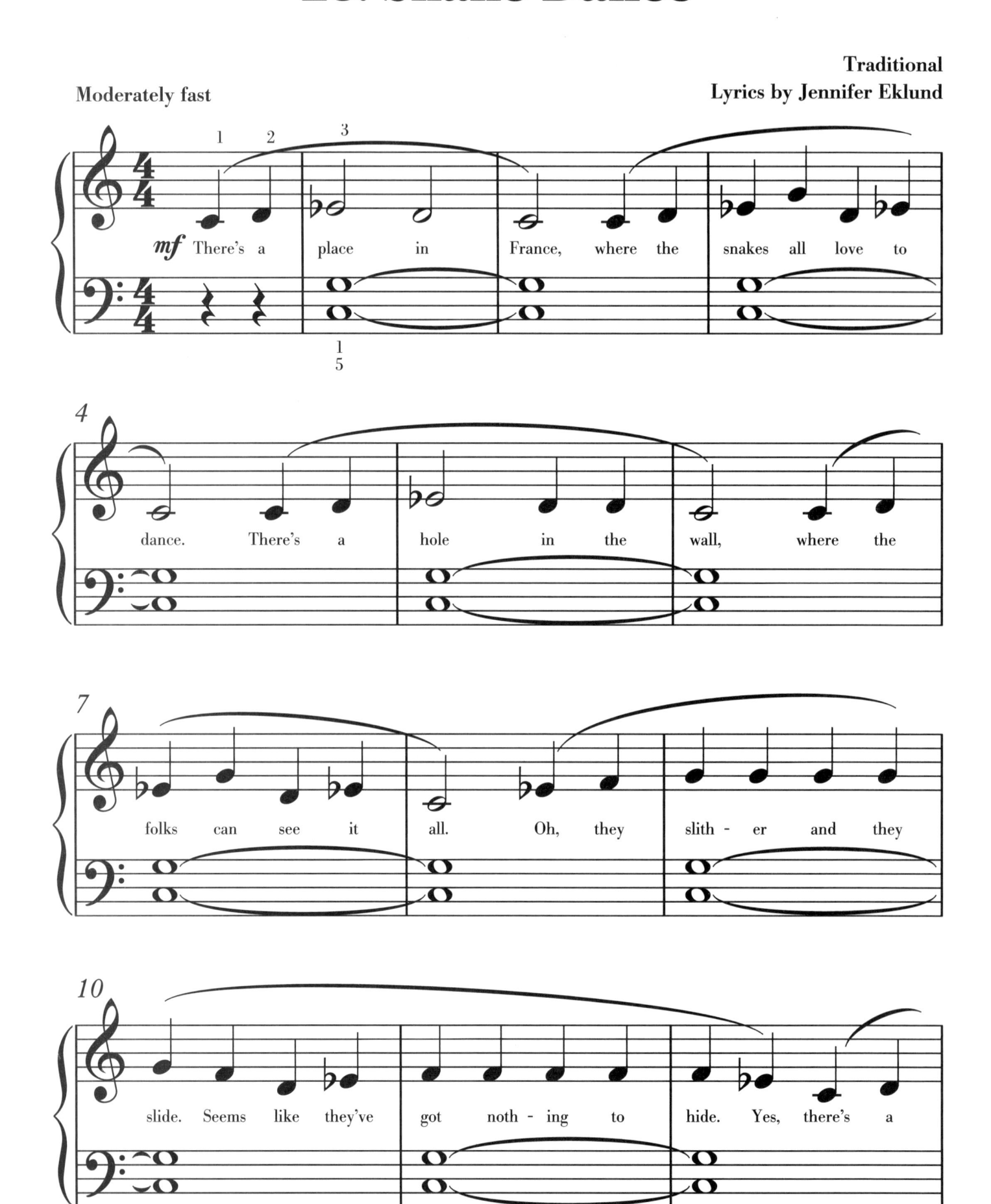

Traditional
Lyrics by Jennifer Eklund

Moderately fast

mf There's a place in France, where the snakes all love to dance. There's a hole in the wall, where the folks can see it all. Oh, they slith-er and they slide. Seems like they've got noth-ing to hide. Yes, there's a *place in France, where the snakes all love to dance.* **f** *Oh they slith-er and they slide. Seems like they've got noth-ing to hide. Yes, there's a place in France where the snakes all love to dance!*

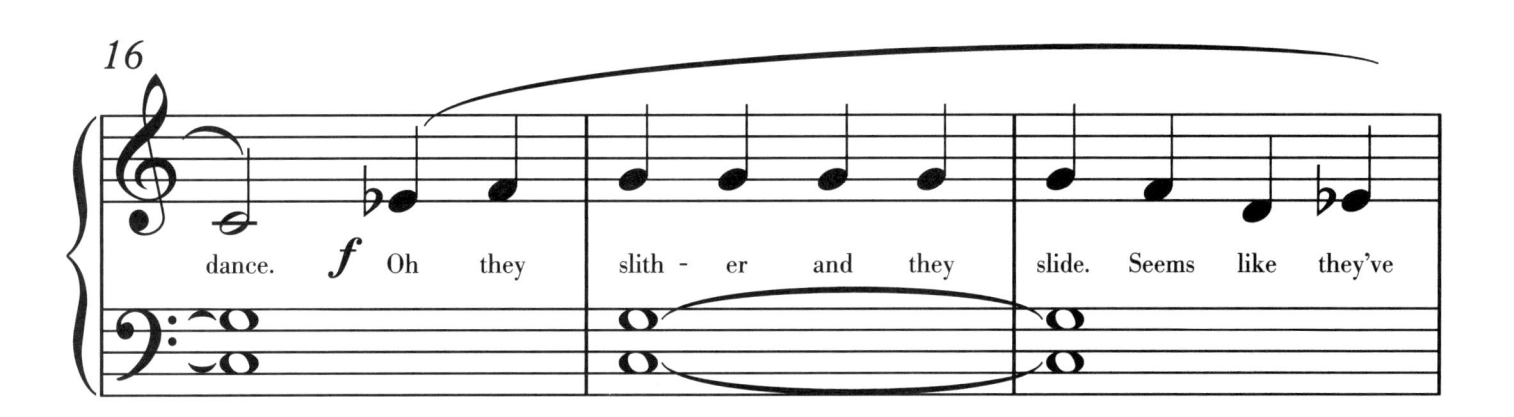

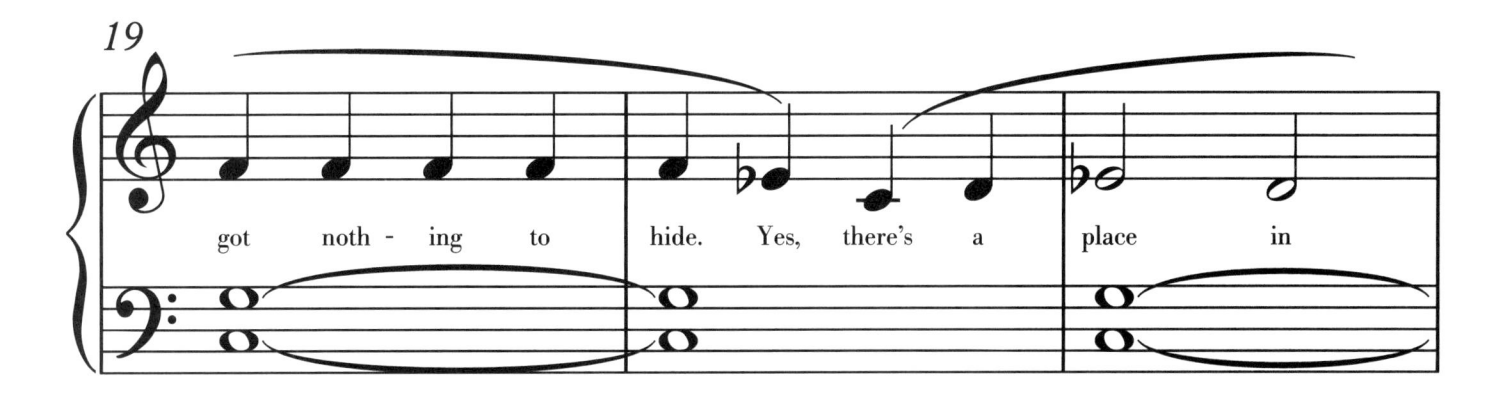

Sharps

♯ = Sharp sign = play the key a half step higher

New Note

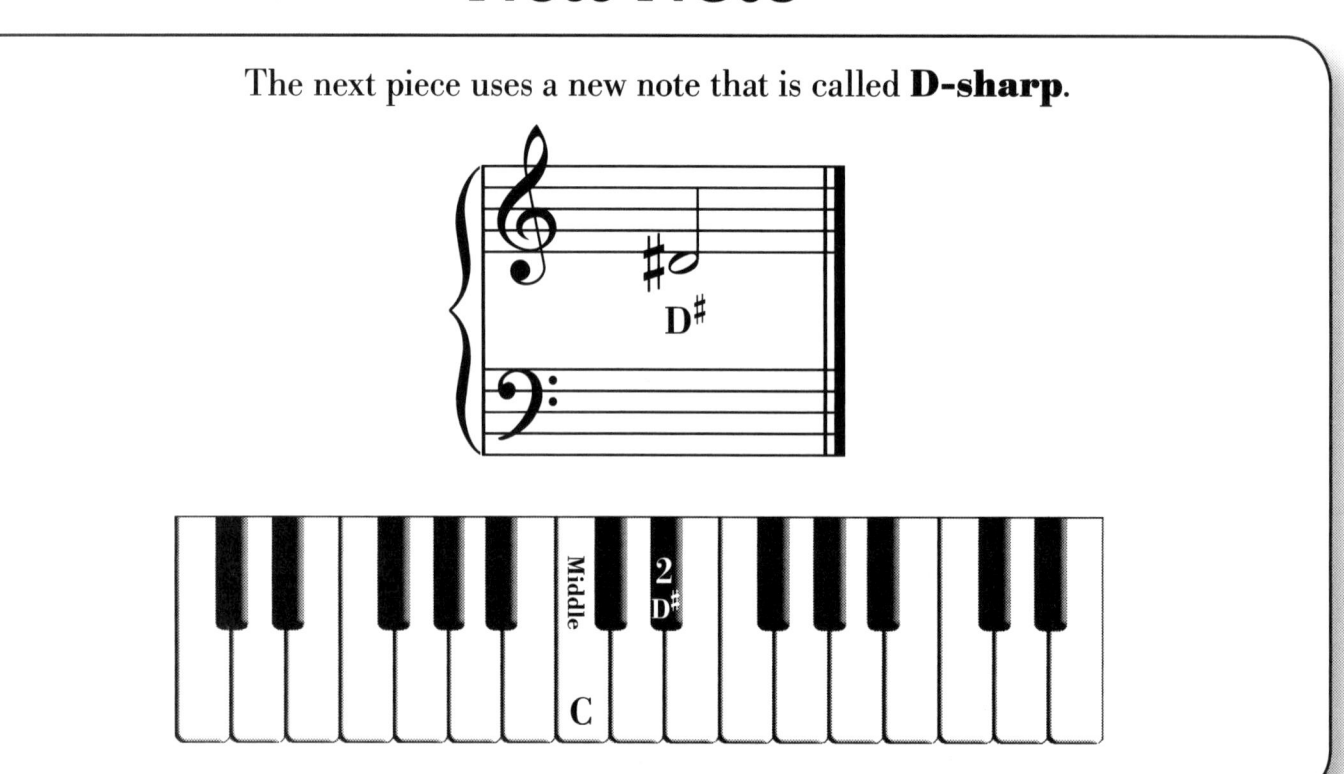

The next piece uses a new note that is called **D-sharp**.

29. Pronto Prep

♪ *Play the example below to help prepare for "Kitty Waltz."*

2 on D-sharp

29. Kitty Waltz

Music & Lyrics by
Jennifer Eklund

Gently

p Sweet lit-tle kit-ty, so grace-ful and light.

Can't we be friends for life? I'll hold you tight!

Sweet lit-tle kit-ty, oh why can't you see?

I think you're as dear as can be!

Copyright © 2015 Piano Pronto Publishing, Inc.
All Rights Reserved | PianoPronto.com

Naturals

♮ = Natural sign = cancels a sharp or flat

Accidentals

Sharps, flats, and naturals are referred to as **accidentals**. Once a note has been changed to a sharp or flat, it stays that way for the whole measure. The sharp or flat sign will not be written again in the same measure.

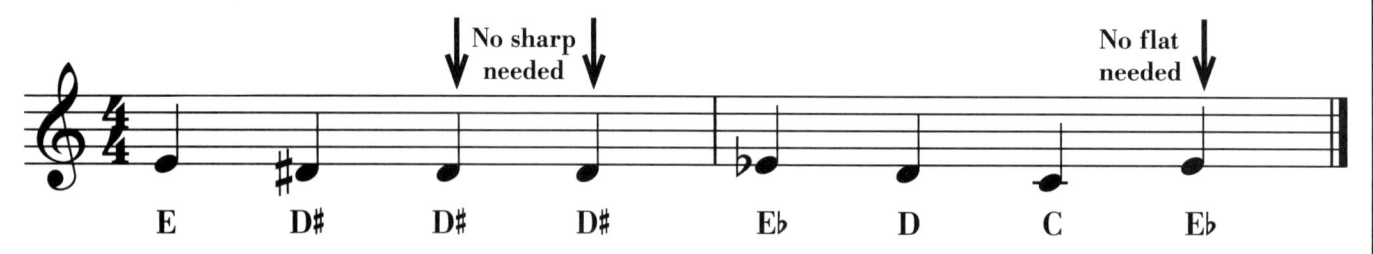

E   D♯   D♯   D♯   E♭   D   C   E♭

Only a **natural sign** can cancel a previous sharp or flat in a measure.

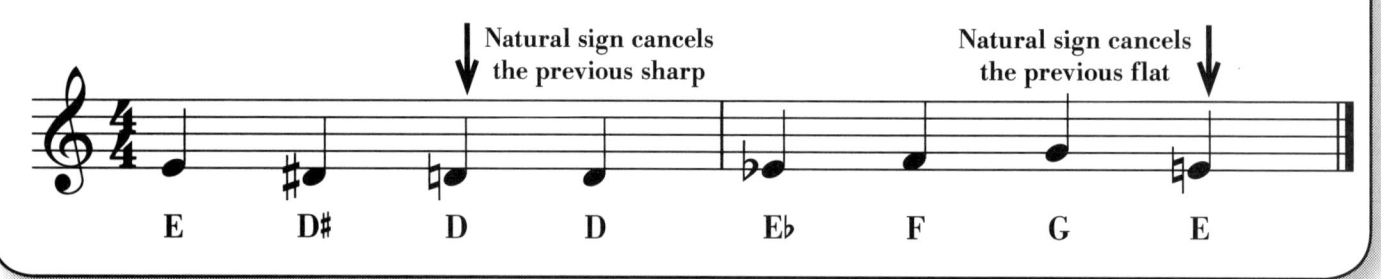

E   D♯   D   D   E♭   F   G   E

30. Pronto Prep

♪ *Play the example below to help prepare for "The Old Gray Mare."*

30. The Old Gray Mare

Traditional
Arr. Jennifer Eklund

New Note

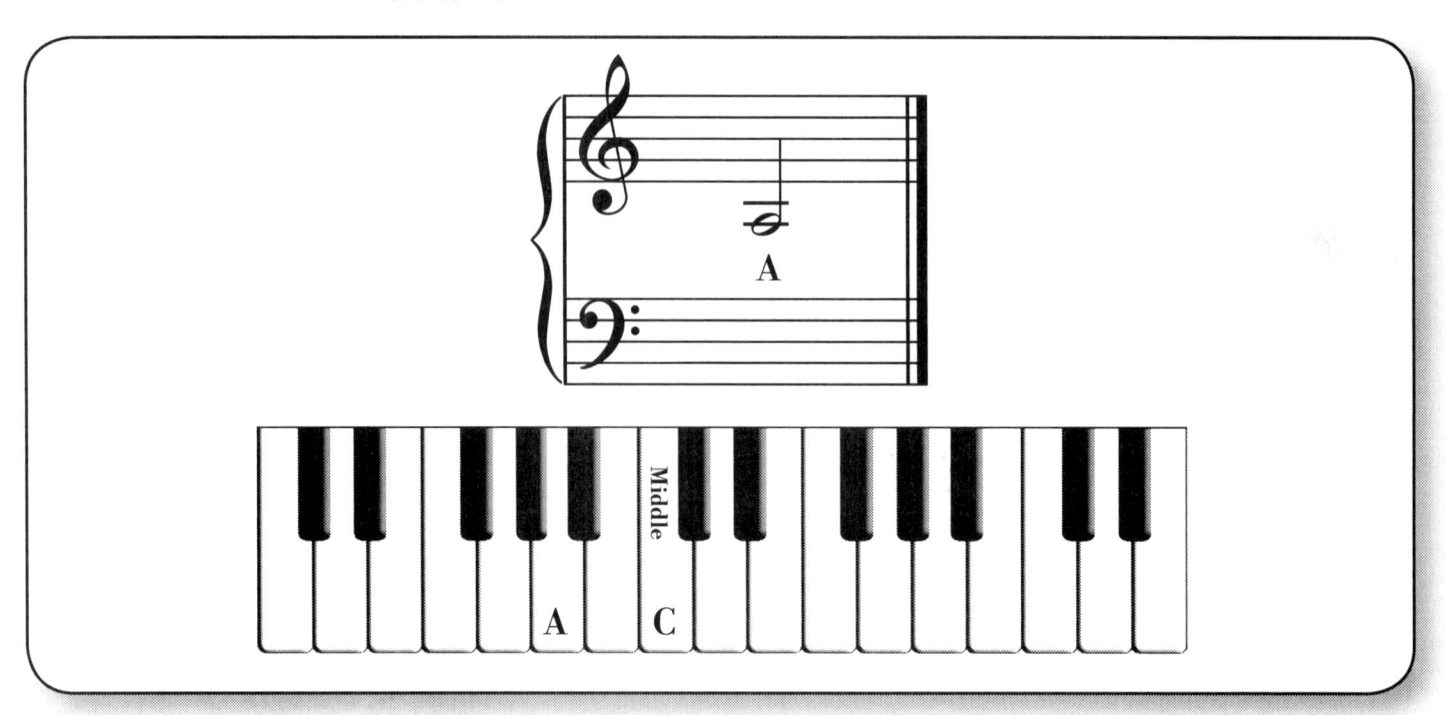

A

31. Pronto Prep

♪ *Play the example below to help prepare for "If You're Happy and You Know It."*

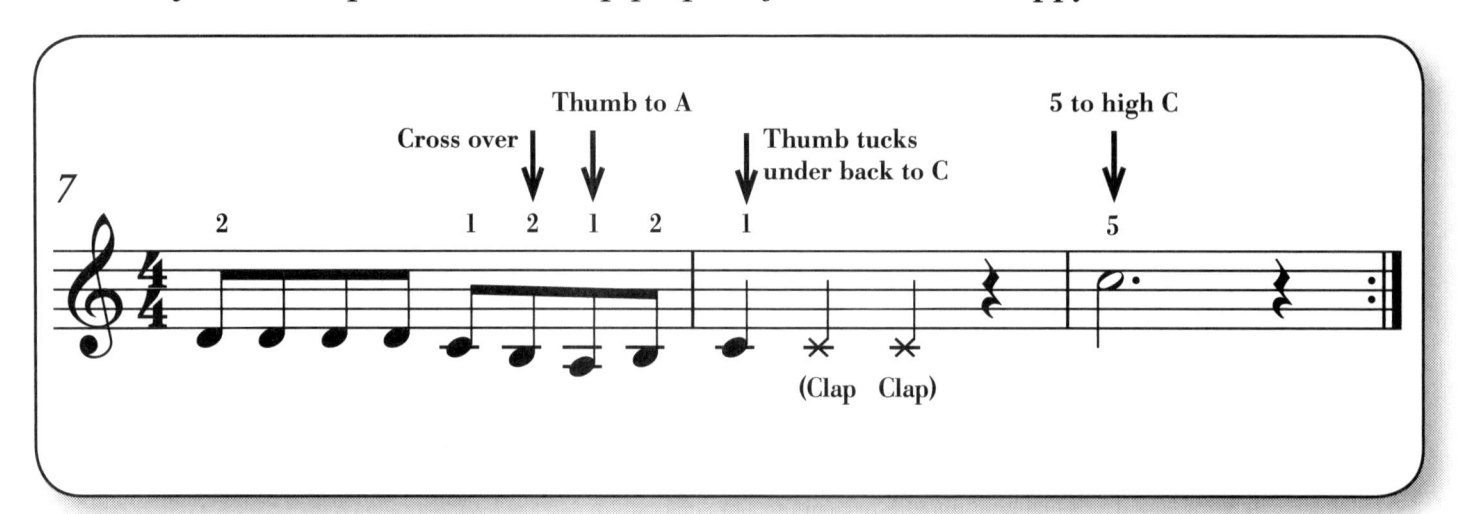

Before you begin:

♪ Label the **treble clef note** in **measure 9**.

♪ Label the **bass clef notes** in **measure 5**.

♪ Does the next piece begin with a **complete measure**? _____

31. If You're Happy and You Know It

Traditional
Arr. Jennifer Eklund

New Notes

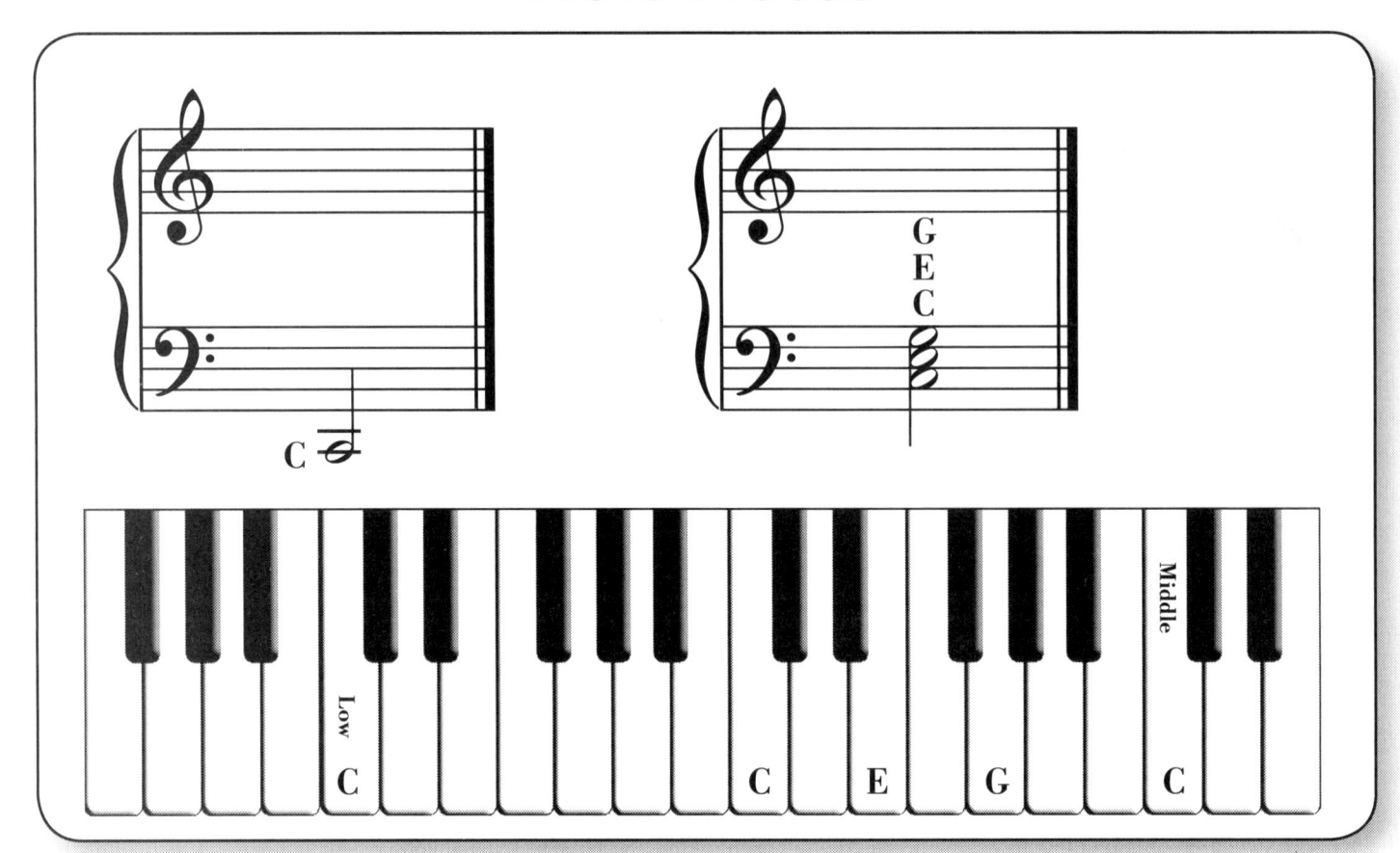

Fermatas

A **fermata** indicates that a note should be held longer than its given note value. Fermatas can be placed above or below a note.

32. Pronto Prep

♪ *Play the example below to help prepare for "My Country, 'Tis of Thee."*

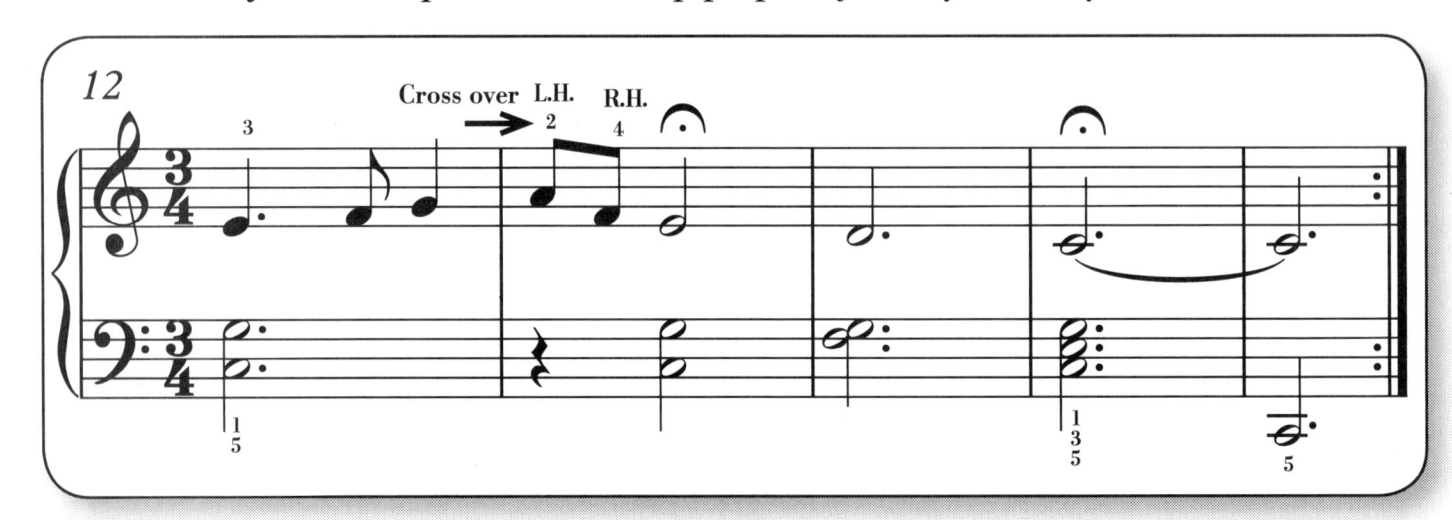

32. My Country, 'Tis of Thee

Traditional
Arr. Jennifer Eklund

Moderately slow

mf My coun - try, 'tis of thee, sweet land of lib - er - ty,

of thee I sing. Land where our fa - thers died,

land of the pil - grims' pride. From ev' - ry moun - tain side,

let free - dom ring!

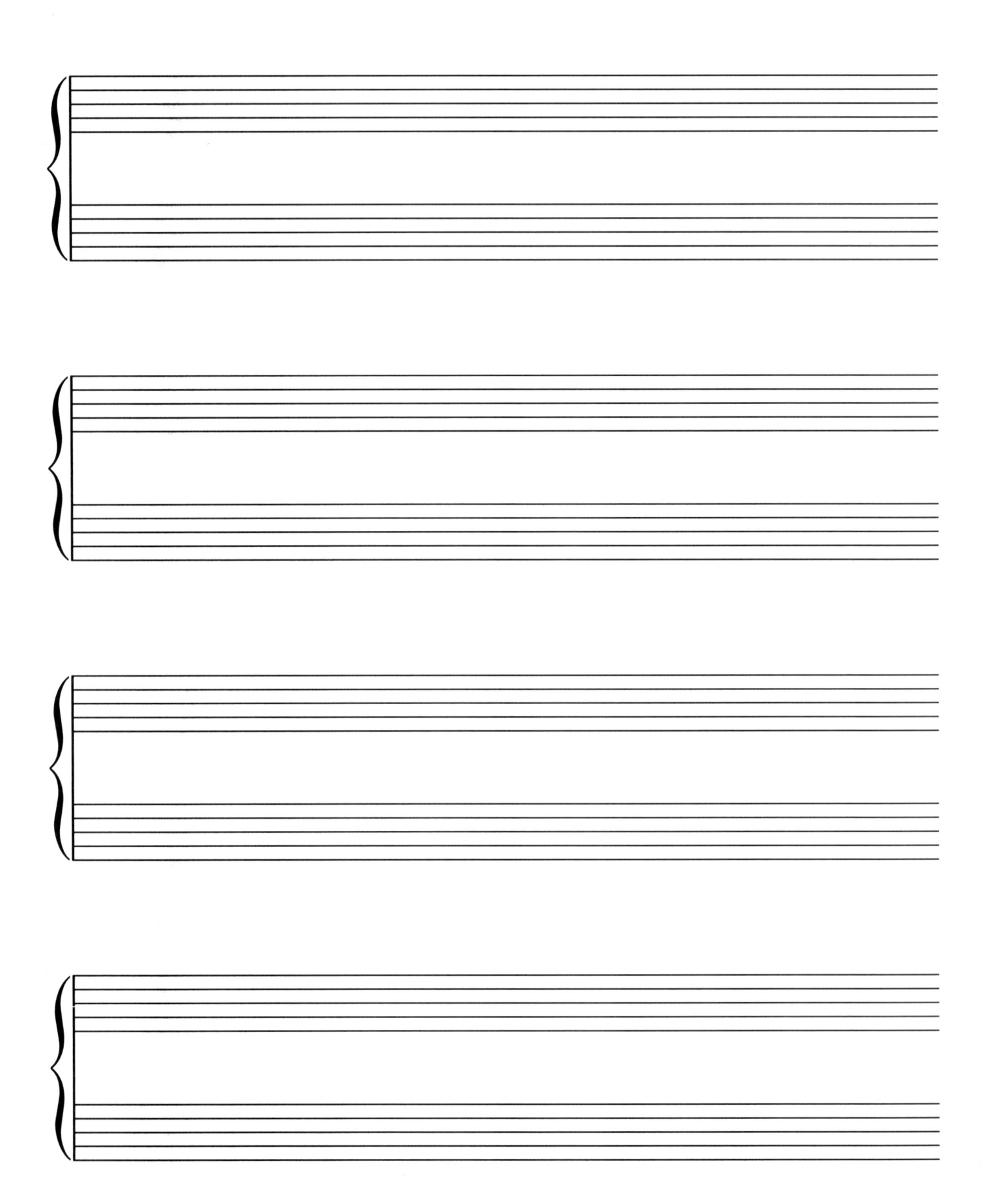

Certificate of Achievement

Congratulations to

_____

(Student name)

for successfully completing Piano Pronto: Prelude.

Date of completion: _____

Teacher signature: _____

Jennifer Eklund

(Author of Piano Pronto)

PIANO PRONTO